MORE PRAISE FOR *Pushir*

"This powerful journey through life is elegantly unfolded by author Terra Trevor. Weaving her personal story through parenting, death, grief and living, she gives readers a glimpse into her soul. At moments, Trevor's story brought to life by her exceptional writing brought tears to my eyes. I could share her heartache and felt the tendrils of joy spring to life as she began her healing journey."

    —Kim Phagan-Hansel, editor of *Adoption Today* magazine

"Terra has woven a moving story of love and heartache across time and culture. She has integrated her own American Indian culture into the dynamics of transracial adoption and described in detail life in a transracial family that has not been done before to this extent. Her courage to describe these events with great honesty, bears witness to a family that provided warmth, encouragement and humor in the face of adversity."

    —Phillip Capper, *Adoption Australia* magazine

"In *Pushing up the Sky* Terra Trevor weaves our interconnectedness with nature, her Native American culture and the culture of her Korean born children to create the sense of permanency, which is so necessary for every family. Trevor demonstrates how interdependencies in families take different forms over time."

    —Kathy Beck

"Accurate and compelling. Terra shares what few understand. I loved this book."

    —Gigi McMillan, Executive Director, We Can Pediatric
    Brain Tumor Network

"Brave, beautiful, deeply moving, and very necessary. This powerful account of the author's confrontation with all life could challenge her with, gives us the inspiration to persevere with help from our friends as we let the love in our hearts keep us grounded, and smiling. I thought my twenty years as a neurologist had inured me from the pain of my patients. Trevor's book reminded me that there are moments to embrace even through life's most arduous travails."

    —Judy Willis, M.D.

"This is a book to cherish and pull out again and again. Hope is on every page."

    —Maggie Dunham

# Pushing up the Sky

## A Mother's Story

### Terra Trevor

KOREAN AMERICAN ADOPTEE ADOPTIVE FAMILY NETWORK
EL DORADO HILLS, CALIFORNIA

Korean American Adoptee Adoptive Family Network
P.O. Box 5585
El Dorado Hills, California 95762
916-933-1447
www.kaanet.com

© 2006 by Terra Trevor
All rights reserved. This book, or parts thereof, may not be reproduced in any form
without permission.

Cover design by Peri Poloni-Gabriel, Knockout Design, www.knockoutbooks.com
Interior design by Stephanie Billecke

Library of Congress Cataloging-in-Publication Data on file with publisher.

ISBN-13  978-0-9776046-09
ISBN-10  0-9776046-08

First Edition
Manufactured in the United States of America
12  11  10  09  08  07  06    1  2  3  4  5  6  7  8

"Pushing up the Sky" by Terry Trevor, from *Children of the Dragonfly: Native
American Voices on Child Custody and Education, edited by Robert Bensen.* © 2001
The Arizona Board of Regents. Reprinted by permission of the University of
Arizona Press. An excerpt from "Pushing up the Sky" was first published in slightly
different form in *Childhood Brain & Spinal Cord Tumors: A Guide for Families,
Friends & Caregivers,* by Tania Shiminski-Maher, Patsy Cullen, Maria Sansalone.
© 2002 O'Reilly & Associates, Inc. Reprinted with permission of O'Reilly &
Associates, Inc.

## AUTHOR'S NOTE

The title *Pushing up the Sky* is from a traditional American Indian story of the Snohomish tribe which testifies and speaks to the great power of what we can accomplish when people work together with a common goal.

I wouldn't be here without the steadfast support and love of many people.

This is a true story. Some names have been changed.

# FOREWORD

I am honored to have been asked to write the foreword for *Pushing up the Sky*. I myself am a product of multiracial adoption. Through my experience as a "hard to place" child, one of mixed heritage who now identifies primarily as American Indian adopted into a "typical American family" with a father of Japanese ancestry, a mother of Croatian heritage, and a brother adopted from a Jewish family, I can relate to many of the nuances of this memoir. Being taken away from my birthparents by the state at fifteen months old, I was bounced from home to home within the foster care system for two and a half years and finally adopted at the age of four. I was in need of a loving and stable family who would be in my life, long-term, to help build trust and object permanence, developmental skills usually learned in formative years through consistent parental bonding. As a young adult I needed to find my biological roots, my point of origin and fill the hole that was missing in my being. This need to search was not a reflection on my adoptive family, I would not have been the person I was (nor would I be now) without them. It was more for closure, for being able to finish the first leg of the trip confident in where I came from and in who I was, so that I could forge ahead on the rest of the journey.

It takes special people to step up above numerous fears, to care for children who are not their own, as their own. But it takes even more loving and courageous people to step into parenthood knowing that their adoptive children have extra needs, especially in the area of psychological and physical medical attention. When I was adopted, in the early 70's, there were no services that eased children and families through adoptive transitional times. Now, it's recommended that families go through family therapy and the Trevor's learned that this was important to the overall well-being of their family. It is crucial that children have a forum in which to express themselves and understand that their parents are listening and willing to step into action. Over time with this, trust and cooperation are built and children become more content and confident within the family structure. Not only is family therapy a need for children within the adoption system, but many are also in need of medical attention.

A condition of my adoption was that the adoptive family would have to provide open-heart surgery due to a hole in my heart, from birth. Without this surgery I would not be here now, so my adoptive parents also gave me the precious gift of life. Each day since making that revelation, I praise the Creator, our Lord, for my mother and father and their selfless giving to a child that they just began to know. Like my parents, the Trevor's also stepped up to meet the ongoing medical needs of their adoptive son. The willingness to take a risk by adopting a baby needing medical attention shows that unconditional love outweighs fear and can produce abundant joy.

Ultimately, this book is about finding identity and searching for a place of belonging, as individuals and as a family whole. It's also about breaking free from fear and stepping into life in its entire splendor.

Terra and I have known one another for years. As people open to sharing life's experiences, we bonded not only over our shared American Indian heritage, but also on a deeper level over how adoption has touched our lives and transformed our being, our center. I'm overwhelmed by her family's life experiences and appreciate all of the facets in which their strength and faith carried them through. It takes courage to revisit ones life and even greater courage to write it down for others to see. Terra does a beautiful job in detailing this memoir with clarity, color, and depth.

Each child within this life story had different needs, including their biological child, and it was important that these needs be addressed with where each child was in their own development. I applaud Terra and Gary for listening to, recognizing, and responding to the needs of their children. Most importantly, for understanding early on that their children never gave up their rights to cultural connection or biological information. They went to all lengths, laying down any self discomfort or adoptive parent fears, to make sure their children had access to their culture and biological information and were also accepting to bring them into their own cultural heritage.

This book is full of valuable insight and is one that will touch the heart and reveal our human capacity to love through a variety of experiences. I pray that it will move you through thought and into action, into recesses of grief and joy, and into a newfound appreciation for all parties involved in the adoption process; the biological parents, adoptee, and adoptive parents.

LESLIE KODA

# ⇄ FALL, 1972 ⇄

"I want to cancel my appointment," I told the woman at the front desk. "Instead of birth control counseling I need a pregnancy test."

The doctor at the Free Clinic rubbed his beard. "If you don't have any money you'll have to apply for welfare." He scribbled an address and phone number on a piece of paper and handed it to me.

The next morning I phoned social welfare to make an appointment and was told they didn't give out appointments. Interviews were on a first come first served basis. The route to the office was only five miles away. The building was a colorless 1960s block of concrete. At the reception counter, under bad fluorescent lighting, I filled out the forms. The clerk took my paperwork and motioned for me to sit down.

"Number thirty-two," the social worker called out. I was number fifty-six. My shorts were soaked with sweat, and my bare legs stuck to the orange plastic chair. The room was filled with women and crying babies. I thought of my mother at age fifteen, pregnant with me. Finally my number was called. I was led into a windowless office. The social worker lit a cigarette, and smoke poured from her nose like a dragon.

"Are you giving the baby up for adoption?" She asked. The question unnerved me. She eyeballed me up and down and hissed, "You've written down that you're Indian—if it was going to be a white baby it would be easier to find a family to adopt it."

I clenched my jaw to stay calm. Brown haired and green eyed, most strangers didn't place me as Indian, but the baby I hadn't meant to create was more Indian than white; the father of my child-to-be was a full blood.

This was my first glimpse at the way race and culture collided in adoption. For the first time I realized I'd been passing as white whenever it suited me, and that my baby was not white, and that I'd never be white again.

The social worker looked at my stunned face and shook her head. It was 1972, I was a nineteen-year-old, unmarried college student, and pregnancy caught me unprepared to become some-one's mother.

Though we spoke occasionally on the telephone, my relationship with Richard was over. It had ended weeks before on a windy night in Arizona under a climbing moon. The next day I headed home to California. Underneath my embarrassment about repeating the family cycle of unplanned teenage pregnancy, especially when I'd been so determined not to, there were moments when I smiled as the baby swelled within me. But I was certain I was not ready to be a mom. Or was I? Before I made a decision, however, I miscarried. At least I did not have to surrender my child to another.

TWELVE WINTERS LATER, IN 1984, I sat in the lobby of Holt International Adoption Services. The room was decorated in pastel wallpaper, with a nubby textured sofa. This time I was married and on the receiving end of adoption. Within the next twenty-four hours my husband Gary and I were due to become the parents of a one-year-old Korean boy.

As our son Jay grew up I knew he would wonder about his Korean birthmother. I might never get the chance to meet her, yet I know she must be generous, patient, joyful, and loving because Jay turned out to be all those things. I like to think his birthmother is a lot like me, but was forced to make a decision that I did not have to make.

I had a profound knowing-feeling when the telephone rang the day we received Jay's adoption referral. I was outside watering sprouting morning glories, and before I answered the phone I knew it would be the adoption agency telling me about my soon-to-be child.

Four months later when Jay was placed in my arms, immediately I understood something was far beyond ordinary about him. He was calm and centered in a way that let you know he possessed a great amount of wisdom; his presence made skeptics believe in angels. There was something extraordinary about the trauma that surrounded Jay's life and how he eased his way through it. He was born with a medical condition called syndactyly, which caused the bones in his fingers to be connected together making his hands look like tiny mittens.

Jay came home to us a few days after his first birthday, weighing only sixteen pounds. He was small, chubby, gentle, cheerful, and the most angelic looking baby anyone had ever seen. In the daytime, while I did housework, he was happiest to be on my back in a baby carrier, or to ride across my chest in the orange soft cloth carrier he arrived from Korea with. When I spoke the handful of Korean words I knew; his face glowed with joy. Each time I put him down on the floor he crawled around on his hands and knees, following me around the house. If I left a room without letting him know, he'd frantically search for me, and when he finally located me, he'd wrap his arms and legs around my knees and hang on like a baby bear locked to a tree. It took weeks before he would allow me out of his sight.

Our biggest hurdle was that Jay wouldn't let anyone other than me hold him, including Daddy. Gary was patient, willing to coax him into being held for a minute or two. It took a month, a large amount of patience and a box of animal cookies before he allowed Gary to hold him when I was in the same room.

Since I'm Native American, naturally we had first looked into an American Indian adoption. However, the Indian Child Welfare Act of 1978 (ICWA) requires efforts be made to place American Indian children with birth relatives, then with tribal members, and then with families from other tribes. To apply with the Native American Adoption Exchange I needed to provide an enrollment number or certificate of degree of Indian blood. While ICWA is needed to reduce the movement of Indian children into non-native families, the requirement of enrollment is like having a pedigree and, ironically, another barrier Native Americans have to face. The only proof I need is my grandfather's word, and the law leaves me able to give birth to a child who would fall under ICWA jurisdiction, and yet I was not Indian enough to adopt an American Indian child.

After researching other domestic adoption possibilities available within the United States, none of the alternatives felt right to

TERRA TREVOR

us. Next we decided to explore the international options. As the son of an Irish immigrant, Gary also has a strong ethnic identity. In 1927 at age 24 his father left Ireland and moved to America. While he cherished his newfound life in California, his heart also beat for Ireland, and he passed this love on to his family.

Because of our strong cultural roots it was important for us to be able to generate a heartfelt connection to the culture, customs and people of the country we chose to adopt from. But we were limited to those countries, which allowed for adoption in the United States. Of those we could have chosen, South Korea caught our attention.

Usually infertility prompts couples to pursue adoption, but I have never walked the infertility treadmill. When Gary and I decided we wanted to become parents, I got pregnant without any problems, then gave birth to our daughter Vanessa in 1981. The pregnancy and birth were trouble free and easy, yet when we decided to add more children to our family we chose adoption. We were positive we wanted to adopt, not to serve a social cause, but simply to raise another child.

We chose adoption over pregnancy because we wanted to make a difference in this life by parenting children who were already born, waiting, and needing a family. We chose South Korea; a county bursting with orphanages. We chose a Korean baby with medical problems enough to cause him to be labeled special needs and difficult to place because deep down inside I knew adopting children who were waiting to be matched with parents was my calling in life. When I shared this with Gary he said, "I've got that same feeling."

Jay endured the first syndactyly-release surgery when he was eighteen months old, and the process involved skin grafting, with grafts taken from the soft skin near his groin area. Every few months he underwent another surgery to separate another finger, and by the time he was three years old, he had ten perfect fingers. We had taken a risk by adopting a baby with a medical situation requiring corrective surgery, but the amount of joy Jay brought us outweighed anything else.

We were eager to adopt from Korea again to add a third child to our family. This time we weren't following the birth order: Our newest child would also be our oldest.

# ⇒ SUMMER, 1987 ⇐

It was one of those days. I couldn't wait to get home from work and change my clothes. A heavy July fog rolled in, and I was so tired I decided to put on my bathrobe. After dinner my husband Gary sliced watermelon. It was my turn to wash the dishes. What could it possibly hurt, I thought, if I left the dirty dishes sitting on the table for a while? We generally kept our house clean, yet on this day the rest of the house was a mess, with sandy beach towels, the picnic basket and cooler from a pleasure-filled weekend strewn in the hall, so I decided to let the kitchen go too. What I really wanted to do was read my book.

Six-year-old Vanessa twirled around the room in a see-through lilac chemise rescued from a rummage sale box. She was wearing lipstick too, and blue eye shadow reached past her eyebrows.

Three-year-old Jay was still potty training. He could take off his underpants five hundred times a day, but never once would he get them back on again himself. Sometimes I let him go bottomless. That's how he was on this particular evening, playing on the floor with little cars. Eyes filled with brown warmth peeked out from under a cap of shiny dark hair; it was the kind of black that looked red in sunlight. His underpants, however, were nowhere in sight.

While I relaxed in the untidy living room, nose in my book, the doorbell rang. Gary answered the door.

"I'm from the adoption agency," a male voice said. "I live a few blocks from here, and thought I'd drop by on my way home from work and meet you."

I lurched bolt upright. The wood floor felt gritty on my bare feet. Before Gary got a chance to offer our visitor a seat, I heard the back door bang, and in bounded our six-month-old Newfoundland puppy. Her bark had a friendly woof in it. All sixty pounds of her romped in circles around this man I had not yet met.

Out of the corner of my eye I saw the cat leap on the kitchen table and start licking one of the bowls. A garlicky smell from the pot of chili verde I'd cooked for dinner drenched the air. I was grateful I'd picked a huge bunch of fresh daisies that morning; perhaps the flowers would catch the social worker's eye and keep it off of the cat. Fortunately this was our second adoption, and we knew surprise visits were not part of the procedure. The man from the adoption agency was only trying to be neighborly by stopping by instead of phoning. He talked with us for few minutes, and said he would call us sometime within the next week to set up an appointment. Then he left.

GARY AND I HAD BEEN MARRIED for eleven years. We made a good team. His mood was constantly changing while mine was predictable. He provided me with variety, and I provided him with consistency. I was the budget-balancer, and he believed in creating abundance. We were both thirty-four with a thirst for adventure and had spent the last six years of our marriage as parents. Now we were ready for a third child. This time we were both less than thrilled with the prospect of adopting a baby. We wanted to add another child to our family and continue to go camping without diapers and car seats, so when we got the telephone call telling us about seven-year-old Kyeong Sook, we said, "Yes."

## ≷ WINTER, 1987 ≷

Kyeong Sook was due to arrive at the airport at nine o'clock in the morning. Waiting for the plane to land my heart raced. *A child I'd never met was about to become my daughter.* The only thing we knew about her was from a brief summary provided by the adoption agency. It didn't tell us much other than she was small for her age and had the mannerisms of a much younger child. She liked to play outdoors, loved babies, and she was talkative, cheerful, and well liked by the orphanage staff. Her background history, however, was sketchy. The photos showing a petite street-wise looking girl with dark determined eyes sent off warning bells that I had ignored.

I'd managed to get security clearance and was able to walk up the long passageway and board the Korean airliner. My gaze bobbed among the people still on the plane, searching, hoping to recognize my new daughter.

Our eyes met. She was much taller and bigger than I expected. I wondered if perhaps she'd had a growth spurt in the four months since receiving her adoption referral. I spoke with her escort and checked the wristband she was wearing to make sure, and I found it said Kyeong Sook Trevor.

How should I greet a new child? Should we hug and kiss? How would she greet a new mother that she'd never met before?

"I'm your new American mother," I said pointing to myself, speaking in my slowest, most careful Korean. I gave her a light hug and felt her small body go rigid. Thick, black hair curved slightly below her chin, framing glowing round cheeks with dimples. She had a box of chocolate candy and was popping pieces into her mouth. I took a deep breath and tried a few more of the phrases I'd managed to memorize in Korean. "Are you thirsty?" I asked. She stared at me with dark brown eyes, and her head moved up and down. So far pretty good: we could communicate. I slipped her hand in mine, and we went searching for a drinking fountain. Then we made our way through the long customs line. Gary, Vanessa and Jay were waiting for us near the exit.

"She's tall for a seven-year-old." Gary said.

At six, Vanessa was one of the tallest girls in her first grade classroom, yet she was a whole head shorter than Kyeong Sook.

Vanessa grabbed her new sister by the hand. "We bought you a new Barbie with long black hair, and you have a new bed and a red bedspread, just like mine." She was not the least bit concerned that her new sister didn't speak or understand any English. Vanessa was delighted with the idea of getting a sister. In the beginning she was a tiny bit worried over the fact that her new sister would be almost a full year older than she was. Then Vanessa warmed to the idea and had been looking forward ever since.

Kyeong Sook turned to Jay and began chattering in Korean. Even though Jay looked unmistakably Korean, his gestures, mannerisms, and most of all, his command of English said that Jay was an American boy. Having been adopted as a baby, he never learned to speak Korean. His eyebrows curved in upside down smiles, four-year-old Jay welcomed his new sister by offering her gum, piece after piece.

Weeks earlier we'd mailed Kyeong Sook a small photo album filled with pictures of our house, our dog, and us. She pulled the photo album out of her plastic carry-on bag and showed it to us. All three kids looked at each other and laughed, Gary and I laughed too, and the ice was broken.

Before we faced the long drive home we stopped for hamburgers. "Cola" and "hamburger," it turned out, were the only English words Kyeong Sook knew. She opened her burger, inspecting its contents, flipping the beef patty on the table in a way I might have done if I'd found a rubber sink stopper inside. With a wan look on her face, she put the meat back inside the bun and took another bite. One sip of Coke sent her sneezing and gasping for air.

Our home was a single-story house, on the central coast of California, a mile from the ocean, with rattan furniture and hardwood floor simplicity. Our house was on the edge of a city neighborhood that boarded a rural area. The back door opened with its characteristic squeak, the yellow tile against white walls made the sunny kitchen glow. The room was ice cream melting hot. Winter slipped back into summer. All three kids threw off shoes and socks, leaving me with a jumbled pile in the doorway. They ran through the house in a way that Vanessa and Jay usually didn't, all rules abandoned. The toilet flushed four times, doors slammed.

Kyeong Sook washed her hands with the faucet running full force. She dumped the soap out of the scallop seashell we used for a soap dish and said something to me in Korean. White soap was caked into the grooves of the shell and she scraped it out with her fingers as she spoke. When I failed to answer, she repeated the phrase louder.

Only the Korean word for mother rang out to me. I got out the English-Korean picture dictionary. She paged through it and pointed to a picture of a seashore and then to a picture of a fish.

"Ocean. Mother. Fish." I said in Korean. Her eyes shone like two high beam headlights lighting up a dark mountain road, and she showed me how her mother scraped fish out of shells.

When dinner was being prepared my new daughter opened the refrigerator and inspected the contents. She pulled out the jar of *kimchi* I'd purchased especially for her and gave me a quizzical look. Then she searched through my pots and pans and found my rice cooker. At the table, as I bent my head over my bowl of pinto beans and corn bread, I watched her load her bowl with rice ready to loose herself to her appetite. She seemed happy to eat whatever we gave her, but she was happiest with rice and *kimchi*.

After dinner Kyeong Sook offered to help me with the dishes, and she set about the task in a specific manner. Two plastic tubs I seldom used were taken out from under the sink and filled with water. The dishes were first rinsed in one container, and then she washed them in the other. After each piece was carefully dried, she twisted the dishcloth in a decidedly foreign spiral.

Kyeong Sook crossed her arms on her chest. She looked up at me with serious eyes, like someone who was used to being in charge.

"I'm not really seven. I'm ten," Kyeong Sook said. Her eyes were like two black stones. She shifted uneasily, and the color drained out of her face.

I stood quietly listening, blinking. I don't know how I managed to understand since she spoke in Korean, but I was positive I heard correctly. Gary and I looked at each other, and I kept trying to talk myself out of believing what I thought I had just heard.

While a nervous knot formed inside my stomach, Gary telephoned our friend Kathy who spoke Korean. I sank into the deep cushion of the sofa, and Gary and Kathy talked on the phone.

A half hour later Kathy came to our house and spoke with Kyeong Sook. My guess was correct. Our new daughter was really ten years old.

Kathy questioned Kyeong Sook further. Her expression was grim. "She said her mother told the people at the orphanage she was seven, and she promised her mother that she would never tell anyone that she wasn't."

"Tell her we don't care how old she is." I found myself saying, "Make sure she understands that we want her, and that her age doesn't matter."

After letting out the truth, Kyeong Sook began to relax. With our friend still translating, she told us stories about her life. In Korea she had lived in multiple foster homes, and it was her job to keep house. She made the rice, and did all of the clean up too. At ten she had already begun to shrug off childhood, not believing it could ever belong to her. The day her mother brought her to the orphanage and told them she was seven, was the day her childhood really began.

ALL EVENING FRIENDS AND relatives dropped by with welcome home gifts for Kyeong Sook. Yet not wanting to overwhelm us and barge in on our first night together, each person stayed briefly and then left. When the last guest of the evening was gone, Kyeong Sook brought out the Korean-English dictionary. She pointed to the word "famous" in Korean. Then she pointed to Gary. With her face pinched into a question mark, next she pointed at me, and then she pointed again at the word in Korean that means famous. She wanted to know who was famous. She thought someone must be famous in our family and that's why so much attention.

As best he could, Gary tried to explain that all the fuss was for her, and that our friends were happy she was here.

"It's not fair," Jay whined, "Why is she getting so much stuff?"

Vanessa tossed her waist length hair in a huff. "Yeah, how come there aren't any presents for us?"


A FEW MINUTES LATER GARY discovered three identical wrapped packages left on the table. One had a card with Vanessa's name on it. The second package was for Jay, and the third, of course, was for Kyeong Sook.

After opening her gifts Kyeong Sook was less guarded, and we watched her sense of humor and imagination emerge. She began playing a make-believe game that we did not understand. She spoke in rapid-fire Korean:

"Mom *toe gee*—rabbit. Dad *sah sum*—deer." Kyeong Sook teased in Korean. Then with a belly laugh she added, "Jay *goh yang ee*—cat."

Jay began meowing like a kitty. Although he did not know how to speak Korean, he knew the word for cat from studying the English/Korean picture dictionary. Her joke suited his quirky sense of humor that always made me laugh.

"What's Vanessa?" Gary asked.

"Yeah, what am I?" Vanessa questioned.

A sly grin spread across Kyeong Sook's face.

"Vanessa—*twae ji*."

I gave Kyeong Sook a sharp look. My comprehension of Korean was a bit better than she thought. *Twae ji* means pig, and being called a pig in Korean has the same meaning as it does in English.

When Vanessa learned that Kyeong Sook called her a pig, the smile on her face vanished like sunlight slipping behind a cloud.

"She's ten Mom." Vanessa groaned, "Not seven like we thought. This is a serious mistake. How could you do this to me?"

I pulled Vanessa onto my lap. "All sisters tease." I said. "The difference is your sister teased you immediately, on the very first day, before you had a chance to get to know each other." I told Vanessa things would be rough at first, and that it would take awhile, but eventually it would get easier.

Kyeong Sook's eyes followed my every move. She watched me hold Vanessa, watched in a way that made me feel uncomfortable. I had no idea why I felt uncomfortable, only that I did. It hit me then that since the girls shared a bedroom, I wouldn't be able to talk with Vanessa alone before I tucked her in bed. It was our nightly ritual. Each night, first I tucked Jay in and spent a few minutes alone with him. Next I would tuck in Vanessa, and we'd chat for a few minutes. Now both of my daughters would be sleeping in the same bedroom, side by side in twin beds.

When Vanessa went into the bathroom and began squeezing a line of toothpaste onto her brush, I followed behind her, closed the door and sat down on the edge of the tub and talked to her more about her new sister's unexpected older age. Within five or six minutes Vanessa began to calm down enough so that she would be able to fall sleep.

When I walked out of the bathroom I could feel Kyeong Sook's eyes bearing down on me.

We tucked the children into their beds, and Gary and I kissed them each good night.

"Sweet dreams," I said.

Gary and I retired to our bedroom. I collapsed in my bed and wrapped the quilt around me, feeling crazy tired, but my mind hummed. I was filled with joy and filled with fear. Gary pulled me close to him and the next thing I knew it was morning.

# ⇝ WINTER OF SETTLING IN, 1987 ⇜

The next morning Gary was up at the first dim light, moving quietly in the dark house. He has always bought me time to sleep at the expense of his own. The moon had gone down and only a few stars blinked. I lay there watching the first sunlight catch the tops of the trees, while Gary chopped kindling; I smelled smoke from the wood-burning stove. I got up then; the smell of coffee drew me out.

I peeked into the bedroom Vanessa and Kyeong Sook now shared. They bounded out of bed the moment they saw me. When Kyeong Sook skipped down the hall towards the bathroom, for the briefest moment it felt like it did when Vanessa had a friend spend the night. It hit me then, how does a mother get used to the idea of acquiring a ten-year-old literally overnight? I didn't feel like I was ready yet. It was just like when I hadn't felt ready when Vanessa was born. Whether I was ready or not, it was happening.

"Can we have cocoa for a special treat?" Vanessa asked. I looked at her rapt face. Her brown eyes were shinning. She turned toward me. "Well, can we Mommy?"

I nodded. "Do you want a marshmallow on top?"

"Come on," Vanessa called to Kyeong Sook from behind the closed bathroom door. "Mommy is going to make cocoa for us."

Next I walked across the hall to check on Jay. He was lying on his back, wide-awake. The window shade was up, and the room was filled with pale morning light. He glanced at me, then shut his eyes tight, and pretended to sleep. I turned to leave, and he whispered, "Mom, when you see my eyes open early in the morning, don't say anything to me because I'm busy thinking."

I went into the kitchen. Gary was starting to make breakfast. A minute later Vanessa and Kyeong Sook's high pitched voices arguing interrupted my first sip of coffee. I bolted out of my chair. Gary motioned for me to sit down.

"They have to learn to work it out on their own." He said. I settled back and wrapped my bathrobe around my knees.

"Give me my slippers," Vanessa screamed. Her voice was cold and flat, filled with a warning that sent us running into the bedroom. Jay was out of bed now. All three kids were on the floor. Kyeong Sook's feet were stuffed into Vanessa's new blue fuzzy slippers. Vanessa was clutching the slippers, trying to pull them off.

"Your feet are too big, and you're going to stretch them." Vanessa screamed. "Jay, come help me."

In a blur Gary and I saw Jay and Vanessa trying to pull the slippers off of Kyeong Sook's feet. But Kyeong Sook was stronger than they were, and she managed to lay flat on her back on the floor and brace her feet against the wall. When she did this, Jay lost his temper. His face turned bright red.

"Take off my sister's slippers," he demanded.

Gary reached towards Jay to pull him back, but he reached too late, and we watched as Jay's teeth sunk into the soft brown skin on Kyeong Sook's stomach. Then Kyeong Sook began screaming. For a moment I held her rigid body trying to comfort her, but she pulled away from me. Vanessa slumped into my lap like a rag doll, all the emotion drained out of her. Gary held Jay as his body shook with long wailing sobs.

When he was a toddler Jay had a biting problem. When he got mad, instead of using words to deal with a situation, his first reaction was to bite. We worked to help him move beyond this phase by giving him lots of positive praise when he expressed his anger verbally. It had been well over two years since he had bitten anyone. I thought the problem had been resolved, and now I knew it wasn't.

There had been little competition between Vanessa and Jay. Most of the time they adored each other. Neither one of them had ever experienced overt hostility, either with each other, or with anyone else, so they were shocked by the reality they were plunged into. By the look on Kyeong Sook's face I guessed this might be the first time she had faced overt hostility too.

All at once we discovered there would not be a honeymoon. Our amalgamated family life together began immediately, and it hit us full force. Once again I had that same sense as when company or the cousins came for an overnight stay. When the children had overnight guests the activity level peaked, and my emotions rode on air currents as I paced my way through the visit. Yet with company or cousins I knew it would eventually end, and once they left I could settle my children down, and we'd go back to our regular lives. Only I couldn't because these were all my kids.

In a desperate attempt to establish some semblance of order and routine, Gary set a platter of pancakes on the kitchen table. He had made real pancakes; the kind made from flour, oil, eggs and buttermilk. There was a faraway look in Kyeong Sook's eyes. She scanned the breakfast table. Then she got up and pulled the jar of *kimchi* out of the refrigerator. I helped her scoop out a helping of the garlicky, red-peppered cabbage and placed it in a bowl on the table next to the syrup.

Jay cut off a hunk of butter and mashed it on top of his stack of silver dollar pancakes. I watched my son hold his fork between his index finger and middle finger; a maneuver that would have been awkward for me, but Jay was able to pick up each bite of pancake with excellent dexterity. This unusual control of finger movement and some light scarring were the only telltale signs of his original syndactyly.

We didn't think Jay would be displaced by the event of adding another child to our family since he was still the youngest and the only boy. Gaining another older sister, especially one who was also Korean, we hoped, would just add more wealth to his life. Yet, of course, Jay was going to be displaced. How could I ever have thought he would not be. We were all were going to be displaced, at least for a little while.

After breakfast I consulted our kitchen calendar, which was the nerve center of our household, and I cancelled the majority of my commitments for the next couple of days. It was Friday, and Gary had taken a vacation day so that he could stay at home. We spent the day getting acquainted with Kyeong Sook and keeping our lives as low key as possible, settling in, finding our rhythm as a family.

Usually Gary went to work at seven in the morning, and on weeknights he didn't come home until seven at night. By the time he got home Vanessa and Jay already had dinner. They would have already had their baths too, and Gary would arrive while I was in the middle of reading a bedtime story. Instead, all day that first

Friday and Saturday after Kyeong Sook became a member of our family, Gary stayed home. Rather than do his regular weekend chores, he hung out with the kids and gave them much more attention than usual. Yet Kyeong Sook didn't know any of this, so she probably thought her new dad was always home.

"Daddy, tell us a Myrtle and Marvin story." Jay and Vanessa begged.

"After dinner, after your pajamas are on and your teeth are brushed," Gary agreed.

Myrtle and Marvin stories were a favorite with the kids. It was a tale Gary made up. Myrtle and Marvin were seagulls, and they had two seagull children. They lived in the cliffs near the ocean, and each night Gary thought up an elaborate adventure involving the seagull family. On the nights when Gary was too tired, the stories were short. The first Myrtle and Marvin story Kyeong Sook heard was one of the longest and most detailed stories ever. That night Myrtle and Marvin became the proud parents of a third seagull child. Jay and Vanessa sat with their eyes riveted on Gary while he told the story. I'm sure Kyeong Sook didn't know what Gary was saying, but it was clear she was happy, wearing her new pajamas, sitting next to her dad on the couch, with a grin on her face.

The following morning when I walked into my daughter's bedroom I was greeted by a complicated tangle of clothing. Jeans, skirts, sweaters, shoes; all of these things had been removed from the closet and tried on by Kyeong Sook. She was getting to know our household, one closet at a time, in the predawn hours while the rest of us were asleep.

"You're up too early," I said. "Are those my old rain boots you're wearing?"

TERRA TREVOR

Kyeong Sook grinned at me. "Up too early," she said.

The next day we found her rummaging through the house again before the sun was up. Each time I said, "you're up too early," she giggled and repeated the phrase. She carried the English-Korean picture dictionary with her at all times, and she began to learn English much faster than we thought she would.

OUR FIRST WEEKEND TOGETHER raced by. On Sunday afternoon a Native American ground blessing ceremony, an event I had been looking forward to, was scheduled to take place at a nearby community gardens. Because this was a new garden plot, before the rows of winter vegetables were planted, first the earth would be blessed.

I brought Vanessa, Jay and Kyeong Sook with me, and we arrived a few minutes late. A small crowd of Native people had assembled, and the ceremony was about to begin. I made eye contact with my friend Jean and she motioned for us to join her near the front, so that the kids would be able to see.

The ceremony began. A number of the elders were dressed in traditional regalia. In the quiet of the afternoon, below a blue sky and goldenrod blooming against sienna earth, while one of the elders offered a prayer, Kyeong Sook began whimpering. She tried to hide behind my back. That day I had no idea what was bothering her, and I brushed it off as typical childhood shyness. After the ceremony was over, Kyeong Sook skipped off to the playground with the other kids, and I talked with some of my friends. By the time we got home, the episode of Kyeong Sook whimpering and trying to hide behind my back was forgotten.

When Monday morning came it was time for us to get back into our regular routine. Gary went back to work. Vanessa and Jay were dropped off at school.

I wasn't working at the time and had planned to keep Kyeong Sook home with me for another week or two before starting her in school. She was in the process of learning so many new things. We didn't want her to feel like she needed to learn everything all at once. So, while Vanessa was off at school in the first grade, and while Jay was at the preschool he attended three mornings a week, I got to know my new daughter's personality and tried to understand why she was the way she was.

To my amazement Kyeong Sook didn't enjoy staying home and having me all to herself, something Jay and Vanessa could never get enough of. She told me stories in Korean mixed with broken English that I was not always able to follow: Slowly I begin putting the pieces together. Kyeong Sook never attended school in Korea. She was taught to read and write at home, and every year her mother told her that she would go to school the next year. But every year was the same; she never started school. She told me this story often, always telling a slightly different version. Each story gave me new insights.

"I wait and wait for America school, but America just like Korea."

Immediately I took Kyeong Sook to our neighborhood elementary school, and let them know that she barely spoke English, and that she would be starting school right away. Fortunately the principal and teachers were warm and welcomed us.

Kyeong Sook was placed in an ESL classroom with children who spoke Spanish and were learning English as a second language. She enjoyed the structure and organization of school and liked school days better than weekends. Yet getting dressed for school was filled with heartache for Kyeong Sook and headache for me. First she pulled on a pair of gray sweatpants, and then she switched to jeans. Fifteen minutes before it was time for us to leave, Kyeong Sook put on a pair of green shorts. She handed me a rubber band. "Ponytail," she requested. I struggled to get her chin length hair secure.

She stomped her foot, and snapped the rubber band out of her hair. "No. Long ponytail, like Vanessa."

"Hey, those are my socks." Vanessa pinched at Kyeong Sook's feet. "Mom, make her take them off."

Kyeong Sook sat firmly on the rug and rooted her feet into the floor.

"Honey, let's go find a pair of your own socks." I pulled her by the shoulders, her leaden weight surprised me; she was an even match for my stubbornness. Next I scooped her around the waist and tried to lift her up. I pulled with all the might of my five-foot-two, 108-pound frame, but she locked her arms around the leg of the coffee table.

Vanessa might as well have asked me to put the kitchen stove on my head; it would have been easier than getting Kyeong Sook to take off the socks.

"In Korea I have one shoes, two dresses and no pajamas. Only sleep in clothes." Kyeong Sook said.

I'd stocked her dresser drawers with a five-day supply of clothing and it overwhelmed her.

"What Kyeong Sook wear?" she asked each morning.

It didn't matter which outfit I suggested, she was able to come up with a reason against it. I didn't care what she wore but I was unable to avoid conflict over clothing selections.

"Do you like dresses or would you rather wear jeans?" She pointed to Vanessa's lavender sundress.

"Don't let her wear my dress." Vanessa pleaded. "Why does she always want to wear my clothes?" Even though Vanessa's clothes were much too small for her, Kyeong Sook constantly begged to wear them. No matter that I tried to prevent it, Kyeong Sook often sneaked out of the house wearing something belonging to Vanessa.

"Mommy don't let her do it again," Vanessa begged. "Please." Her voice quavered.

Washing clothes, folding, hanging up clothes, all of this I did night after night. The next day the laundry piled up again. A friend suggested I temporarily remove all excess clothing and leave Vanessa and Kyeong Sook just the basic items they needed.

The next morning, Vanessa, bleary eyed, swaddled in an afghan, crept near my bed and whispered, "Hey, I looked all over the bedroom, and in the bathroom hamper too. I know there's suppose to be more clothes in my chest of drawers."

The oversized bedroom stenciled with flowers and hearts on one wall, and cars, boats and trains on another, was divided up to make it suitable for both girls. The old double dresser, which had magically transformed Vanessa from baby to big girl when I presented it to her at age three, immediately lost its dignity when it had to be shared with her new sister.

Vanessa blinked back tears. "You've ruined my life."

"I know it's been hard for you getting a new sister who turned out to be older than we expected."

"You said she'd be seven, and little like me, but she's practically as big as you are Mom, and she acts like a baby, a great big baby."

I wholeheartedly agreed with Vanessa that it wasn't fair, not for any of us, but what was a mother to do?

Vanessa's view of herself placed her as the oldest sibling. She had complete confidence in herself as oldest child and big sister. Then we brought in Kyeong Sook who usurped her position and knocked the world as Vanessa knew it to smithereens.

Jay was no longer biting out in anger, yet he was being much quieter than usual, and this worried me. I resisted my urge to rush him through his breakfast and hurry off to get him to preschool on time. A red-tailed hawk sat on a tree branch outside our window. It was the biggest hawk we had ever seen, and we let ourselves be late so that we could see its enormous wingspan as it flew away. After twenty minutes, the hawk still sat on the branch, and Jay sat perfectly content watching him. Suddenly I realized I was watching a bird sit on a branch, instead of *waiting* for a bird to fly away. Jay, ever the fun-loving, joyful child, sat beside me keeping his eye on the hawk, barely daring to blink. I memorized the moment and saved it in my heart.

After that I did my best to spend a few minutes alone each day with each child. Usually during our alone time, Jay cuddled on my lap and chewed on the corner of his blanket. When Vanessa and I were alone, she ranted and raved and scratched at the top of her head until her hair was a wild mass of tangles.

Kyeong Sook sucked up time alone with me in a way letting me know she viewed family life similarly to how a pack of wolf puppies maneuver. She jockeyed to be alpha, and she made it clear when she felt reduced to omega.

It was becoming painfully clear that no matter how much I loved children, it was far more difficult than I imagined to form an immediate bond, and to transform another mother's child into my own. Into our lives had walked a half-grown kid, our kid, demanding to know why the other children had bathing suits in the bottom dresser drawer.

"Yes dear. Your brother and sister needed those last summer. Don't worry, when the weather warms up we will buy you a bathing suit, too." Daily, Kyeong Sook cried over not having a bathing suit. The bathing suit issue stood in center storage in her mind, a metaphor representing all of the losses she'd experienced in her life. She didn't believe that I planned to buy one for her. All winter I repeated, "The stores do not have bathing suits yet, but just as soon as they do, I'll get one for you."

# ⟫ SPRING, 1988 ⟪

Finally I spotted bathing suits in the children's wear department in a local store. I purchased a navy blue tank style for Kyeong Sook. Each morning Kyeong Sook peeled off her pajamas and put on her bathing suit. Then she put on a pair of jeans and a shirt. I didn't want her to go to school with a bathing suit underneath her clothes, but I let her do it anyway.

We filled our afternoons carving out sandcastles and collecting seashells. The shoreline stretched back to where it blended with a strand of eucalyptus trees. I leaned back under a bead-blue sky and let the gentle sunshine soak into my flannel shirt, the tang of salt and sea air settled around me.

Jay silently drove a yellow dump truck under my knees, he crawled along, truck in hand, careening through a pile of sand next to Kyeong Sook, slowly winding his way until he dumped a large rock out of the back of his truck next to his sandcastle.

Vanessa raced towards the surf; her body was tall and lean, and her face was angular like Gary's. But instead of his fair ruddy complexion, she was medium-skinned, like me, with straight hair, like mine. I rubbed all three kids with suntan lotion; the white creamy lotion melted into Jay and Kyeong Sook's warm brown skin.

I pulled off my jeans, stretched out my legs, and wiggled my bare toes in the sand.

The wide-open spaces of the beach forgave all wrong doings. When we were at the beach the kids played happily together, and we spent many afternoons next to the pounding surf.

## ⁼ SPRING, 1988 ⁼

Every year our Native American community held a pow wow. It was a weekend I looked forward to. Usually we stayed all day on Saturday and camped overnight. That spring, however, being a mother required my unremitting attention. I was exhausted.

"This year couldn't we just go for the day?" I suggested.

Both Vanessa and Jay gasped at once.

"Can we at least stay until dark?" Jay begged.

"Can I still get an Indian taco for dinner?" Vanessa asked.

The pow wow arena was only a twenty-minute drive from our home, so Gary said, "We can stay for dinner and watch some of the evening dancing, and then we'll drive home."

When we got to the pow wow, Kyeong Sook immediately began whimpering. And when my friends Jean and Tim, dressed in full regalia, came over to talk with me, the moment Kyeong Sook saw Tim with his porcupine roach on his head and two feathers attached in a spinner, she screamed out loud. It took a lot of doing to calm her down. After talking with her for over an hour in the car where she felt safe, I discovered the source of her fear. It turned out what she knew of Indians was based on portrayals she'd seen on television in Korea of America's first people as belonging to a savage bloodthirsty culture. Finally I was able to convince her that the movies she had watched on television were not real. I explained that those were made up stories, and that even in the old days Indians didn't live like that.

Kyeong Sook agreed to get out of the car, and then she saw *real Indians* buying ice cream for their children, Indian fathers holding sleeping babies, mothers braiding their children's hair. She saw happy Indians, laughing and joking with each other.

Later in the evening, after Tim had changed into jeans, she grew so comfortable with the idea of being with a band of Indians, she began hopping around making T.V. Indian war whoop sounds.

"I wanna Indian feather," Kyeong Sook begged.

My friend Jean took charge in a grandmotherly way and said, "Child, Indians don't have feathers. Birds have feathers, I'll get a bird feather for you to wear in your hair."

It wasn't a joking matter. On top of needing to help Kyeong Sook learn American culture from the dominant white point of view, being a member of our family meant she would also need to learn how to move within American Indian culture.

Soon she grew comfortable with the handful of friends we knew living a traditional lifestyle. As long as certain Native American markers were present, she knew what to expect and how to behave. Yet my closest friends were urban Indians like me, living in houses and driving trucks like ours, working as teachers. They were regular moms and dads who went to back-to-school night, just like we did.

Kyeong Sook was fascinated with the topic of Indians, but she was unable to grasp the idea of Indians being Indians unless they were dressed in beadwork and feathers.

## ≳ SUMMER, 1988 ≲

Although my mom and dad adored Jay and were doing their best to fall in love with Kyeong Sook, they were worried about our future. My dad kept saying I had no idea what I'd gotten myself into by adopting Asian children. My mother said Korean children needed to be raised around Korean adults. I knew my parents were right, and concerns simmered in the back of my mind. Feeling rooted in American Indian ethnicity was important to me, and I expected Korean ethnicity would be important to my kids. But I didn't have a plan, and I wasn't sure exactly how to blend Korean ethnicity into our lives.

Soon after adopting Jay, Gary and I had begun to make friends with other parents in our town who had also adopted children from Korea. Originally we first met the other parents through a Korean adoption support group, and from there our friendships grew. We had exchanged phone numbers and soon began getting to know some of the other families better on a personal level. Over the previous four years close-knit friendships had formed, and some of these families had become our closest friends.

We continued to attend the more formal bi-monthly adoption support group meetings, and in addition a small group of families took turns gathering in each other's homes on regular basis. In the winter we met for potluck dinners indoors. While we parents sat in the living room talking around the fireplace, drinking wine and laughing, our kids played together. Our friends' children ranged in ages from four to eight. Everyone except Vanessa, and one other girl, was adopted from Korea. There was one boy Jay's age, and they were particularly close. The girls in the group out numbered the boys. Each time we got together there was a total of at least eight to ten kids. In the summer we got together on a monthly basis for swim parties and barbecues. Soon a tradition of camping together each summer for a weekend at the beach became a favorite family activity.

Gary and I had wonderful fun with this bunch of friends, but it also felt odd to be socializing with a group of all white parents, all with Asian children who were raising their kids as white-alike, in white enclaves with little or no access to other Asians. It was a constant reminder that my parents had good reason to worry about us.

Some of the adoptive parents we knew bought into the line of thinking that it wasn't all that important to raise their kids around other Asians. They believed the alternative, of not being adopted and living in an orphanage was far worse than being raised outside one's racial group. I did not share their views. In my mind the problem with this rationale was the price the kids would pay was their racial identity. I was concerned about the harm I might be doing to my kids since we had few Asian friends, and I wondered why the others weren't worried as well. But this was my very first experience socializing within an upper middle class, all-white group. It was also my very first experience socializing with adoptive parents of Korean-born kids. I was too intimidated to disagree with the opinions dominating the group. I would stir up controversy today, but I didn't have the confidence to do it then. Some were outspoken and clung tightly to their own opinions. Whereas I was lacking the assuredness to tell others that my gut level intuition, and my mom and dad's common sense, went against the early 1980s dogma, which claimed it was OK for white adoptive parents to raise adopted Korean children isolated in white neighborhoods. Gary felt equally as intimidated as I did. He didn't want to say anything either.

Kyeong Sook took an immediate dislike to the adoption support group parents and to their children. From my point of view the problem was, at ten she was the oldest of all the kids, and a head taller. The majority of the girls were seven or eight and closer to Vanessa in age. All of the children were friendly to Kyeong Sook, yet she seemed to feel like an outcast. She worked at keeping herself separate and apart instead of joining in.

When her English language skills were advanced enough to communicate better, Kyeong Sook filled me in on the details.

"Those kids are American," she complained. "I want a Korean friend, a Korean girl, like me." I understood what she meant. Since the children Jay and Vanessa played with were born in Korea and had been adopted into American families when they were babies, they didn't meet her expectations of being Korean.

Our friend Kathy said she knew of a Korean family with a daughter the age of Kyeong Sook. We met the family, and they invited Kyeong Sook over to play. The girls got together a few more times after that, but a lasting friendship did not blossom.

I was delighted when two Korean American families began attending the Korean adoption support group meetings. Instantly the hamburger and potato chip potluck dinners were fused when *kimchi* and *bulgogi* appeared side by side with coleslaw and potato salad. I enjoyed the blend of people and looked forward to these friendships eventually carving deeper than just providing adoption support.

Except some of the adoptive parents did not have much interest in mixing and mingling. Rather than getting to know these new families in the usual way of talking about various topics and finding common bonds, some began quizzing them about Korean culture. It would have been OK if a few questions were asked, and then the conversation was allowed to drift into other areas. Perhaps we could have discovered mutual interests. It wasn't like that. It was more like they were grilling them, and a few of the questions asked seemed too personal.

If that wasn't bad enough, some of the adoptive parents said they saw no need for their children to be exposed to Korean culture, and then an embarrassing silence filled the room.

While I would have loved to know more about Korean culture, I would have preferred to let those new friendships evolve slowly, and learn a little bit at a time. After all, culture is not a thing a person could learn from a conversation. Culture had to be experienced.

The idea of having only a cultural slanted curiosity instead of a desire to build a relationship that would eventually evolve into genuine friendships, struck me as odd.

The tone of the whole situation bothered me. It must have bothered the Korean American families too, because soon they stopped attending the meetings.

Though we didn't know it at the time, we would discover a feeling almost like a code that sent a clear message that it was not acceptable to disturb the racial and cultural comfort level of this adoption support group. For some the comfort zone included occasional Korean cultural activities, and those were the families we continued to form close friendships with, but for many of the parents participation would always be kept at a careful distance.

Gary and I were grateful Jay and Kyeong Sook were growing up with plenty of other children who were adopted from Korea. It was a bonus our kids were rooted within a cluster where Korean adoptees were the majority. But I had to let go of my idea of the adoptive parent group being racially diverse.


EVEN THOUGH MOST OF OUR friends seemed to want to keep interactions with the Korean community set aside for special occasions and not as a part of everyday life, many were curious to learn more about Korean food.

"Where is the nearest Koreatown?" someone asked.

"Los Angeles," somebody else answered.

Everyone let out a deep groan, "It's too far."

"Let's charter a bus," said another.

A number of families wanted to go and nearly every seat on the bus was filled. A banquet room was reserved for us at an elegant Korean restaurant. Three separate tables were set with white tablecloths. We were seated, and menus were passed around. The room was silent. I wasn't familiar with anything listed on the menu. Neither was anyone else at our table, so we guessed and did the best we could. When the waitress took our order there was much confusion. A few minutes later she brought us little dishes of spinach with sesame seeds, bean sprouts and *kimchi*. Bowls of roasted garlic slivers; pan-fried green onions, and lots of dishes of things I didn't recognize were placed before us.

Kyeong Sook grinned. Her dimples deepened.

We sat for a long time, and the waitress did not return. The kids were hungry and began to complain. A person at my table decided perhaps these were the appetizers. Someone else guessed it was the food we ordered. We thought we had also ordered meat dishes, yet none of us knew exactly what we had ordered.

We began to sample each dish. Jay picked up his chopsticks and tasted the bean sprouts. "Good." he said. He reached for a second helping. I watched his thumb and index finger toying across the bowl.

Vanessa sat at the far end of the table with a group of girls, powering down piece after piece of toasted seaweed. Kyeong Sook beamed at me, and dipped her chopsticks into the green onions.

Gary tried the cucumber kimchi and took to it like it was second nature. He poured me more tea, and passed me the roasted garlic. I bit into a clove. Its creamy tang burst open in my mouth. I took another bite.

"Don't Koreans eat rice?" someone asked. A person at my table expressed the notion of rice being a food of lesser status, probably a food eaten only at home, not a dish that would be served at a fancy luncheon. All right. I'll admit it. I actually believed the rice theory might be correct.

As soon as we finished eating, the waitress brought bowls of soup and rice for each of us. Platter after platter of meat arrived. We had ordered four times as much food as we needed. The waitress looked at the empty bowls on the table. A rush of red came to her cheeks. Her eyes moved up and down the table. Every bowl was empty.

The next day I called my friend Kathy. "We made a terrible mistake at the Korean restaurant," I confided. "We ate all of the *kimchi* and vegetable side dishes first; we thought they were the appetizers."

Kathy and her husband invited us to their house for a home-cooked Korean dinner. They had us sit in the kitchen while they cooked so we could watch the meal unfold. We learned in Korean dining there aren't any sequential courses served as in a western banquet. All of the dishes are supposed to be eaten at the same time, and Korean food dishes are served to the entire group and each dish is to be shared by all. They also loaned us a stack of Korean cookbooks, and our formal education into Korean cooking began.

# ⸚ WINTER OF SEARCHING FOR ⸚
## SOUTH KOREA IN CALIFORNIA, 1988

"You never cook Korean food anymore." Kyeong Sook got up from the dinner table and transformed the room into her own inner world. She had been with us for one year and we were at a difficult transition. Lately, she refused to eat a Korean meal when I prepared one, and if I didn't fix Korean foods, she complained about not having them. Aside from preparing a pot of rice and a handful of Korean vegetable dishes, I knew precious little of Korean culture to offer her. It was becoming increasingly clear how painfully ignorant I was.

I wondered what it was like for her to be brought to America, and to become the oldest child in an American family. She had learned to speak English without too much difficulty. Her English was nearly fluent, but she was a stranger in a strange land, desperately seeking a group with which to identify. There were days when she huddled under a blanket, listening to Korean music with the tape cassette player pressed to her ear. Sometimes she fell into loneliness so deep it was as if a series of massive waves hit her hard, without warning. As soon as she caught her breath another wave pounded her under emotionally. At those times only Korean music could console her. She'd sit in the bedroom for hours, until her homesickness lifted. These seemed like typical stages through which she must pass to gain identity in a new culture. Only I didn't have any idea how long this would last.

I could see that it was important to insist that Kyeong Sook learn to think in a new language and adjust to American ways. But I didn't want to erode Korean culture out of her life.

"It wasn't my idea to be adopted, and as soon as I can I'm going back to Korea," Kyeong Sook said.

I kept reminding myself: no child emerges from a troubled past without negative emotional baggage. It's been said that for each year a child is not in your home, it will take the same amount of time after adoption for that child to feel she truly belongs in the family. It was a scary thought. At that rate Kyeong Sook would be twenty-two before things settled down.

Near the end of her first year with us, Kyeong Sook's emotions took a dark turn. She began throwing full-on temper tantrums at least two or three times a week, like a three-year-old might do. It was impossible to tell what might trigger a tantrum. They began like a flash-fire. Then she slammed doors so hard pictures rattled off the walls. She'd lie on the bed kicking the wall, yelling and screaming for over an hour, and then she'd begin crying and this went on for another hour, and she refused to let me comfort her.

A breakthrough came when I burst in on her, ignoring her threats, and I said, "OK, I give up. What did your mother do in Korea when you threw tantrums like this?"

Kyeong Sook stopped crying. She sat up on her bed, and in a clear voice she said, "In Korea my mom didn't know what to do either, and usually she just did the same thing you do."

We both stared at each other. I tried to talk with her about this, but she didn't want to talk. I'm not sure how I had known, but it was then clear to me the tantrum habit had begun long before Kyeong Sook joined our family.

Although she was intelligent, gifted, loving, and a classic beauty, Kyeong Sook didn't realize these attributes applied to her. By the time she became my daughter, she was convinced that she was ugly and stupid and a person no one wanted to be around. On some level I knew she was happy to get new parents. Yet I could tell she also felt permanently trapped. Little in her life in Korea had prepared her for life in America.

I didn't expect her to develop immediate committed feelings for me. I would have gladly settled for patiently waiting until a closer mother-daughter relationship formed in due course. Instead we argued daily. No matter how hard I tried to avoid conflict, I found myself looped into it.

"It's not my fault I was adopted." Kyeong Sook spun around to face me. "I didn't ask to come here. Why can't I just go back to Korea?" She gobbled up the English language fast and put a mournful twist on a well-traveled phrase I often gave my mom while growing up. Only she had an option I never had, there wasn't any way I could have gone back to never being born.

Kyeong Sook stomped her foot. "It wasn't my idea to be adopted. I want to go back to Korea." She aimed her next sentence, "I might as well go back to Korea, because I know you don't want me."

"I do want you," I insisted. Her accusation that I didn't want her shot me in the heart. I did my best to reassure her that I did want her, and she remained convinced that I didn't.

No matter what I attempted, the situation did not improve. Gary didn't understand what I was going through, and he didn't want to talk about it. (He understands now, but he didn't then.) His solution was to work extra long hours to take his mind off things. Often on Saturday's he left the house and went off on his own all day. I felt alone and isolated.

Months passed. The situation with Kyeong Sook got worse. All three kids fought constantly, and home became such a miserable place to be that Gary was no longer able to ignore it.

We began seeing a family therapist. In therapy Jay and Vanessa were encouraged to voice their feelings. Jay didn't talk much in our sessions. He listened and drove his little toy cars along the edge of his chair, and every once in a while he crashed the cars into each other. Vanessa squirmed in her chair and wouldn't talk either. Each week Kyeong Sook cried her way through the session.

Gary and I learned Kyeong Sook's rock-ribbed feelings of anger were a reaction to separation and loss. Much of the outcome hinged on how we allowed and encouraged her strong feelings. It involved pain, and there was no shortcut. We must face the onslaught of intense feelings without drawing back. It was confusing because normal behavior in grief is so different from what is considered to be normal behavior. Grief, we learned, must run its natural course. It is never wise to try to speed up or try to slow down the process.

There were abandonment issues to work through. Each time we began to grow close as a family, and a comfortable relationship settled on the horizon, Kyeong Sook became snappish, angry and unapproachable. Her pattern of throwing temper tantrums that lasted for hours was the way she distanced herself from the rest of the family. It was impossible to find some agreeable ground with her. I knew her behavior was her way of saying, "Don't get too close to me." And unfortunately it worked. It was beginning to be plenty hard for me to work up much affection for her.

In our therapy sessions I learned that it was important to always "be there" for Kyeong Sook. But I didn't know how to "be there" when she kept pushing me out. It was a crazy cycle that wasn't taking us anywhere. I knew the usual rules of conduct in establishing a mother/daughter relationship, but this was more like being in junior high school where you keep trying to work out those difficult seventh grade friendship problems. Kyeong Sook was one of those hard to get along with girls, the kind I steered clear of in junior high. I felt like it would take a team of mothers working around the clock to parent this child.

There were days when I wanted to give up on Kyeong Sook. There were times when Gary wanted to give up too. Luckily we never wanted to give up at the same time. If I was feeling better, he was down. When he wanted to talk about Kyeong Sook. I didn't.

When Gary and I had decided to become parents, it forced our relationship to change. With the arrival of both Vanessa and Jay, after a few months of adjusting, we bounced back a stronger team. The months raced by and I kept expecting any day soon things would begin to settle down.

## ⋛ EARLY SPRING, 1989 ⋚

I was near the end of my rope. It never occurred to me that Kyeong
Sook was at the end of hers. I was in this state of helplessness when
a new idea took life in my mind. I wanted to travel to South Korea
with Kyeong Sook. It was a risk, and I knew it. She was acting out
her fear of being abandoned again, yet I also knew we had to deal
head-on with her desire to return to Korea.

"It's a wild idea, yet it just might work," Gary agreed.

Next we met with our family therapist. "It hasn't blown over," I
said. "Kyeong Sook still wants to go back to Korea. Do you think
it will be OK if I take her to Korea and give her a chance to think
it over?"

There was a long pause. "Well I suppose you can't force her into
this adoption," the therapist said. "I've got to be honest with you,
I've never dealt with anything like this before. Are you prepared for
either outcome?"

I gasped. "Not really."

One thing was certain: Kyeong Sook had been sent off to a new
family in the United States without any real sense of control over
what happened to her. The only way this adoption was going to
work was if she wanted it to.

We couldn't afford a family trip. Besides, this was a mercy mission, not a vacation. Gary and I decided that I should take Kyeong Sook and Vanessa. We hoped the trip to Korea would soften the relationship between our daughters. Vanessa, now eight, had discovered that even though she was much younger than eleven-year-old Kyeong Sook, she held the upper hand in teaching her new sister about American ways. In the beginning it helped Vanessa assert herself. But we didn't want to let this stage go on for too long or it might become a habit. Once when Vanessa was trying to teach her older sister how to carve a pumpkin, Kyeong Sook said, "How do you know I haven't done this before? My life didn't start when I met you." Vanessa needed to grasp that while her sister was new to American ways, her life in Korea was filled with plenty of experiences equally as valuable.

"I CAN'T BELIEVE I'M REALLY going to see Korea again." Kyeong Sook jumped up and down when we told her the news. "If I decide I want to stay in Korea, will you let me?" she asked.

Gary shot a glance towards me.

"We'd miss you if you decide to stay," he replied. Her face brightened. It was clear this is what she wanted to hear.

We talked about the possibility of attempting to locate Kyeong Sook's Korean mother. Yet the decision to search for her Korean mother belonged to Kyeong Sook, and she was against the idea. I knew she would eventually need to reconnect with her first mother, and that she would need time to prepare herself, to get ready in her own mind.

If only we had been better prepared at the beginning of her adoption. We knew very little about the first ten years of her life. Kyeong Sook never knew her birthfather. Her relationship with Gary was her first father-daughter experience. I was mother number two, and all I had to go on was the three-paragraph summary of information handed down to me from mother number one.

I wanted so much to fill up Kyeong Sook's emptiness, to make up for her early wounds, but could I?

Kyeong Sook wanted to return to Korea and live in the orphanage. It didn't make sense to us since she had lived in the orphanage for only a few months. Yet she was driven by a "gotta do it" desire. We were taking the only action we could.

I arranged to get passports, made travel plans, gathered strength, and tried to come up with a backup plan, just in case she decided she wanted to stay in Korea.

# ꒢ SPRING, 1989 ꒤

Vanessa, Kyeong Sook and I arrived at Kimpo airport in Seoul. I'd made arrangements for us to stay at an orphanage instead of a hotel, and the assistant director agreed to pick us up.

"I'll be holding a sign with your last name printed in English," he promised.

I scanned the crowded airport. Vanessa and I were the only non-Asians. At least most of the Korean women were as short as I was, and in the sea of dark brown eyes and black hair, at least my high-cheeked face felt right at home. I was extra nervous because I didn't really speak Korean. My vocabulary was made up of simple nouns and verbs, and I didn't know how to string words together to make sentences.

In a blur of dark hair and dark suits, I spotted our escort holding a bright pink sign that said "Welcome Trevor Family." He was in his mid-sixties, well dressed, formal, and he spoke very little English. He bowed and shook my hand. I bowed. We picked up our luggage at baggage claim, one suitcase each. He led us through the crowd towards the parking garage, and we climbed into his Ford Escort. Wide city streets were jammed with pedestrians, motorists and buses. Little sidewalk shops stood next to skyscrapers. In the middle of five lanes of traffic, an old man on a bicycle with many cartons of eggs strapped to a basket behind his bike weaved in and out of the lanes of cars. We drove through neighborhoods with modern apartment buildings, then into sections of town with traditional style houses with wing-tipped tile roofs. Through the open car window I took a deep breath and inhaled Korea. "The air smells like garlic and sesame."

"It's the *kimchi*, Mom," Kyeong Sook replied. "Everybody makes *kimchi* in great big pots and they keep it outside."

Vanessa wrinkled her nose. "I can smell it in my eyes."

I was caught off guard by the traffic and speeding automobiles. Cars honked and pedestrians leaped out of the way.

We drove to a suburb north of Seoul, in a neighborhood with a small-town feeling. Our driver said something in Korean I didn't understand and let us out of the car directly across the street from the orphanage. We had to cross a narrow street with fast-moving cars.

"When you hear a horn just lean back against the buildings." Kyeong Sook explained."

Vanessa squeezed my arm. "Those tires were only a few inches away from my toes. Why are the streets so narrow?" We trudged up the long cement driveway to the orphanage, through the front gate, and into a playground. Children were swinging; a merry-go-round was spinning at top speed with a blur of black-haired kids leaning into the wind giggling. A teenaged boy on crutches with heavy metal braces on his legs bowed his head in a nod and greeted us in Korean.

"Americans!" The boy's speech was slurred and there was a smile on his face. His feet scuffed against the pavement as he turned to go inside the brick building.

Neither Jay nor Kyeong Sook had lived at this orphanage. It was a small, private orphanage that ran mostly on donations. A close friend of mine knew the director well, and she had called explaining our situation and asked if we could stay at the orphanage for a week. I'd planned to leave a large donation, the same amount of money we would have spent if we were staying at a hotel. I wanted us to experience typical orphanage life, hopefully as close as possible to the orphanage situation Kyeong Sook wanted to go back to.

A few minutes later the orphanage director came out and introduced himself.

He was middle-aged, though he looked much younger, dressed in a dark suit, and his English was perfect. My Korean American friends had given me careful instructions. I said an honorific, formal Korean greeting, adding a slight bow with my head when we shook hands.

He spoke to Kyeong Sook in Korean. Her eyes were transfixed, and she did not answer him. Again he tried to draw her in. She just stood there with her mouth open.

We were led to our room, and along the way we passed a small, square house built of green concrete blocks. The door was open, and the floor inside was a patchwork of assorted linoleum squares. There were rows of girls' shoes lined up outside the front door. We passed a new brick building, and the director explained that this was the new boys' facility. I had seen photos of the boys' old house; it had many holes in the plaster walls, and I knew they had to stuff rags in these holes in the winter to keep out the cold. We passed another humble dwelling. This one was nothing more than a square box of cinder blocks. This house, I knew, belonged to the director. I'd heard rumors that he went out of his way not to live fancy; any extra money always went to support the orphanage.

Our room was on the third floor of the new brick building. We climbed up the stairs and slipped off our shoes, and found Ondol, an age-old radiant heating system, warmed the linoleum floor. Stone flues ran under the floor and carried heat. There were four bedrooms that opened up onto a common living room with a couch, television, telephone, a fan, and a reading lamp. The girls and I were given one bedroom to share, and the other three bedrooms were empty. We were told that other guests might arrive any time. We had western-style beds with rigid Korean-style straw pillows, a western-style bathroom, and a kitchenette we would share with the other housemates.

Our suitcases were loaded with gifts. I knew that Korean cultural etiquette, like American Indian cultural etiquette, requires giving a gift to everyone who showed us kindness. We brought honey, boxes of chocolates, packets of gourmet coffee, tea, hot chocolate, scented soaps, lots of toothbrushes, and the card game Uno for the orphanage kids. Later we discovered that Uno was a favorite and the orphanage deck had been worn paper-thin.

It was dinnertime. I had arranged for us to eat our meals with the orphanage kids. We went to the large room with cement walls painted bright yellow and blue where meals were served. The children filed in. Some of the older kids carried small children piggyback. There were rows of tables and chairs, and the three middle-aged women who did the cooking and serving, grinned and hugged us. Our meal was served on silver-colored cafeteria metal trays, the kind with three dividers.

Kyeong Sook picked up her long-handled spoon. "Rice, soup and *kimchi*. This is exactly what I ate every day when I lived in Korea." Suddenly she dropped her spoon.

"Mom, is this orphanage poor?" I'll bet I was really poor when I was little because we only had soup, rice and *kimchi* everyday; we never had anything else. But the orphanage where I lived we always had soup, rice, *kimchi* and lots of other things on the tables too like apples, sweet potatoes, and yogurt drinks. We even had more snacks than you buy for us in America."

This surprised me. I thought that all Korean orphanage kids ate meager meals.

I was bone-weary. We fell into our beds, and the girls were asleep instantly, but it was a no sleep night for me; I was too excited. I was in Seoul. I had looked forward to someday taking my children to Korea. But I didn't expect to be in Korea under such weird circumstances. I didn't dare plan any ordinary vacation fun out of fear. What if Kyeong Sook wanted to stay here? Our time needed to be structured so that she could glimpse a realistic view of what her life would really be like if she lived in Korea.

Around midnight I opened the window; the moon was lost in a cloudbank, and I could hear high-pitched singing, lilting, graceful, as if the words fell from heaven. The music lulled me, yet I was still awake when the sun rose.

In the morning we strolled down to the orphanage cafeteria and found it was empty, all the metal trays were stacked in rows. We walked over to the orphanage office to see if we could find out what time breakfast was usually served. Funnily I couldn't remember the Korean word for breakfast.

"What time is breakfast?" I said in English. The woman at the front desk gestured helplessly. She said something in Korean, and I didn't have any idea what it meant.

"Kyeong Sook, what did she say?" I asked. Her shoulders slumped. "I forgot."

I urged her to *try* to remember.

I gathered my daughters and we walked towards town. The day before the streets had been jammed with cars and taxis. Now the streets were nearly deserted. We went into a hardware store, at least I think it was a Korean hardware store, but the shopkeeper didn't speak English and he couldn't understand any of the phrases I'd memorized in Korean. Where, I wondered, were all the people? All of the street signs and the writing on the sides of the buildings were in Korean. I was afraid to venture far for fear of not being able to find my way back to the orphanage. So we went back to our room. Back in our room I still didn't know what to do. Kyeong Sook was no help. She didn't know the neighborhood either and she wouldn't translate, so I had no idea how we would be able to communicate with anyone.

I didn't want us to spend the day in our room, but where should we go, and even if I was successful in choosing a destination, how would we get there?

Culture shock had its grip on me; I felt alone and helpless. That's when I began to understand that this must be how Kyeong Sook felt when she came to America.

I wanted to call Gary. He wouldn't know what to do either, yet I wanted to hear the sound of his voice to reassure me I had not fallen off the edge of the world. I opened the phone book to find the code to dial for an overseas number. Or maybe I could figure out how to call the overseas operator and have the call placed for me. The phone book didn't help; I couldn't read a word. I sat down and sobbed. Why hadn't I stayed at the President's Hotel where everyone spoke English, like all my friends had suggested?

"Oh Mommy," Vanessa gasped. "What are we going to do?" My blurry eyes looked up to see eight-year-old Vanessa's bewildered face. She huddled next to me. "Mommy if you can't figure anything out, we're going to have a terrible time." Then her face brightened. "What about the letter?"

My friend Kathy, who spoke Korean, had written me a letter giving me the name and telephone phone number of a woman she knew who lived in Seoul, and who spoke fluent English, just in case I had problems. I pulled the folded piece of paper out of my wallet, took a deep breath, and dialed the number.

The phone rang and a female voice answered. "Yobo Sayo." Uh-oh, I thought. Carefully I greeted the women in Korean, and then all at once I began babbling in English, praying that her American roommate would come to my rescue. The woman laughed. "Yes, I know Kathy." She answered in English and in a distinctly Californian accent, and for the next ten minutes I poured my heart out to her.

She laughed again and said, "First of all, it's Children's Day, and Children's Day is a national holiday in Korea. It's the only day of the year when children are heavily indulged. Korean children usually attend school six days a week. After school and on Sundays, they always study. Today the schools were closed and everybody would be doting on the children. And there is also a taxi strike, that's why the streets are so empty." She encouraged me to call again if I needed further help, and we hung up. The conversation worked as a touchstone for me. It gave me the lift I needed to regroup and the confidence to begin feeling my way through Korean culture.

I managed to locate the orphanage director and learned that meals would not be served in the cafeteria today. Today the orphanage kids had been served a special breakfast in their rooms. A special lunch would be served outside around noon. We were hungry so we breakfasted on nuts and pretzels from my suitcase.

Kyeong Sook slipped her toes into her brand new white tennis shoes without untying the laces, squashing down the heels.

"I'm going to the playground," she said. I watched her walk up to two rosy-cheeked girls and link arms with them. She was culturally relaxed in a way I'd never seen before. For the first time I noticed the delicate bone structure in her high-cheeked face.

The orphanage kids grinned and pointed to Vanessa and said, "American." Then they invited Vanessa to come join them. Vanessa, without any shyness to overcome, linked arms with a skinny, perky girl, who looked exactly like her, except that she was Korean. Their laughter said they had much in common.

Throughout the day the children were offered candy, gum and other treats. Games and contests took place. We were ushered into the church, and the orphanage choir gave a performance. I recognized the soloist from the night before, singing the same high-pitched tune. We watched a talent show in the gymnasium.

The sun began to set, and still the children stayed outside and played. A game of hide-and-go-seek was in process, and Vanessa and Kyeong Sook were in the thick of things. When the sunset gave way to the stars, I brought my daughters inside.

"Look, we've got a new roommate," Vanessa announced. "Beats me who it is, but there is a pair of shoes by the door that wasn't here when we left this morning."

A young woman with long black hair was frying an egg in the kitchen. She introduced herself in Korean. She also spoke Japanese, yet her English was about as limited as was my Korean. We found a high school girl living in the orphanage to translate for us. I learned that she was a student in Japan, and that she was half Korean, half Japanese, and would be living in Korea for a year. Over dark mugs of tea we found a common language by using some pantomime mixed with a little bit of broken Korean that I could understand and a little bit of English. The first thing she asked is my age.

"Thirty-six," I answered. I was beginning to notice that just about everyone I had met so far wanted to know how old I was.

"The reason you are constantly asked your age," she explained, "is because it is necessary in order to determine how to speak to you, how much respect you should be shown."

I giggled. "Some people in America feel it's rude to ask a woman's age."

"Then what's the proper way to show respect?" she asked. I couldn't come up with an answer. "American women want to look young," I replied.

The English-language news was on television. Children's Day celebrations were taking place all over Korea. I began to grasp how important having a family is in Korea and how insignificant orphanage children feel without one. Often in the United States, Korean Americans came up to me on the street and thanked me for adopting Korean children. Usually I ducked out of this by answering in my clearest teacher voice, "I am the lucky one, truly blessed to have been given such wonderful children." I found it a constant battle to help both Americans and Koreans understand that I was not answering a social call. Kyeong Sook was my daughter, and Jay was my son, just the same as Vanessa was my child. I continued to hope Kyeong Sook still wanted to remain my daughter.

## ⤜ SPRING, 1989 ⤛

It was cool in the morning and starting to rain too. After a breakfast of soup, rice and *kimchi*, we set out for Kyeong Sook's orphanage. The director had made arrangements for one of his drivers to transport us. We passed rice farmland, rice paddies with an occasional farmer weeding or plowing. We saw an ox with a farmer leading it. A fine mist drizzled. It was a fast, bumpy ride, and scary, as our car drove quite close to the other vehicles on the road. Our journey took us past small villages. Footpaths dotted the hillside connecting the houses with playgrounds. Women with cloth bundles on their heads walked the footpaths. As we bumped along on the rough asphalt, a couple of times Kyeong Sook mentioned to me that she just *might* want to stay in Korea. Our car turned onto a well-traveled road full of potholes and mud puddles; we passed a dairy farm with Holstein cows.

The orphanage was smack in the middle of nowhere. It was a large modern complex sitting on a large spread of rural land. We were met at the door; we bowed and removed our shoes. Someone bought me a pair of house slippers, the terrycloth kind my grandmother wears. Cola was served. Vanessa carefully pronounced the Korean word for thank you. Kyeong Sook went mute again. I was puzzled. I had no idea why she wouldn't speak or why she wasn't answering anyone. When I questioned her about it, she just lowered her head.

We toured the facility. The moment I entered the building where the preschool aged children lived all shyness left me. These kids didn't care if I had a funny accent when I spoke a handful of broken Korean sentences; they enjoyed all the attention. A small boy about Jay's age, with misshapen hands, tugged at the hem of my skirt.

Since adopting Jay I had learned that there are several attitudes in Korea about people with disabilities that are quite different from attitudes in the United States. In Korea a disabled person is not considered to be whole and is hidden from view and is not expected to accomplish much. It is difficult to find an employer who will hire a person with any type of physical difference, whether it is an actual disability or not. There are not enough jobs to go around, and those individuals with a physical special need have little opportunity. Schools often will not admit a child with a physical condition that differs from the norm. The terms used in Korea "whole person," "handicapped" and "physical defect" convey how little opportunity there is.

With all my might I tried to imagine Jay living in an orphanage home for handicapped children, without any opportunity, without the hope to become whoever he wanted, but my mind did not want to go there. The thought was too painful.

In the building where the older children lived, clusters of women and girls gathered around us. Kyeong Sook was back, and the housemothers looked her over. A fuss was made over how much she had grown. Korean was spoken, yet I was able to guess what they were saying by gestures and simple words I could understand.

Kyeong Sook pulled me into a small office and pointed to a large bulletin board filled with many photographs, "Look my pictures are here." I'd mailed a few snapshots, and they were pinned up on the board along with photos of other children.

"Are these the same beds?" Kyeong Sook asked. "They look so tiny." She walked around the bunk bed. "I remember them being so much larger."

We went into the bathroom. Kyeong Sook showed me a ledge above the sink, where she once placed a dime-store quality, but dearly-treasured, ring her mother had given her. She forgot to put it back on after washing her hands, and when she went back it was gone. And we stood in the spot where she said goodbye to her Korean mother.

I felt the thread connecting me to a women I had never met, to a mother who did her best to raise her daughter and had the courage to let go when the challenge became too difficult, and now it was my turn.

One of the housemothers leaned over and said something to Kyeong Sook in Korean.

"What did she say?" I asked.

Kyeong Sook's face turned a bright red.

I leaned over and whispered. "What's wrong?"

Kyeong Sook took a deep breath. "I don't know, I can't understand them. I guess I don't remember Korean anymore."

"Are you serious?" Vanessa gasped.

"How could you forget Korean so soon?" I questioned. "You've lived in the United States less than two years."

"Beats me," Kyeong Sook said. She let out another deep breath. "I kept thinking it would come back to me, but I can't understand anything anyone is saying."

Suddenly I realized how Americanized Kyeong Sook had become in such a short amount of time.

IT WAS A LONG DRIVE BACK to the orphanage where we were staying. There was plenty of time for thinking and time for talking. I asked Kyeong Sook if she still wanted to stay in Korea. My questions seemed to jerk her mind back from a secret place.

"I'm not sure, I haven't made up my mind yet," she said. Her face looked sad, and instantly I regretted asking. A few minutes earlier a warm feeling lingered between us. Now a wall held together by the fear of not being wanted, stood between us. Vanessa was quieter than usual all day. Suddenly she piped up, and I shushed her before she could say anything. It was warm in the car, the air felt tight, as if there was suddenly less space around us.

I lifted the curtain on Kyeong Sook's memories, and for the rest of the afternoon she greeted the world with total, silent hostility. Her life was torn apart, and I would do what I could to mend it. Think again, I said to myself. This was going to be harder than I thought.

THE NEXT DAY THE director called me into his office. "Do not worry. Your daughter will not want to stay in Korea. Of this I'm positive." I told him that Kyeong Sook was having difficulty understanding Korean. He seemed as surprised by this as I was.

He suggested I take my daughters out to lunch, and he wrote down the address of the restaurant so we could take a taxi.

I called Gary and gave him a progress report. Next I held my breath, consulted my travel book and planned our day. The taxi dropped us off at a rather nice looking restaurant. It was unusual in Korea for a mother and two daughters to go out to a restaurant without a male escort. Inside the restaurant everyone stared at us. Vanessa and I were the only ones who weren't Korean.

I couldn't read the menu, so I asked for *pibim pap*. I had never eaten this dish as yet, but I knew it would be considered a proper thing to order.

The waiter brought us many little dishes filled with *kimchi* and three bowls of octopus soup with tiny legs swirling in the rich hot broth.

Next we were each served a bowl of sizzling hot rice. A raw egg sat on top of rice along with many brown and green vegetables. I pushed at my egg and found a blob of red bean paste underneath.

"Look, those people have the same thing and they are stirring it all together." Vanessa said. I stirred my egg into the steaming rice and I was amazed to discover it sort of cooked right in my bowl. It tasted wonderful.

"Watch out for the bean paste." I told Vanessa. "It's as hot as a jalapeno pepper." Kyeong Sook and I both found hot spicy food to be downright sincere, we liked serrano chilies best, but Vanessa broke out in a sweat just by breathing in the fumes of hot peppers.

I paid the check, and after thoroughly searching, we finally found the restroom.

"Kyeong Sook, how do I use the toilet?" Vanessa asked. At first I thought we were in the men's room. The toilet looked almost like a urinal, only it was completely flat on the floor, yet it flushed like a western-style toilet.

"There was a toilet like this in my house." Kyeong Sook said. I hoisted up my skirt and squatted near ground level. The biggest challenge was not to drop my skirt into the water.

We were having a good time together. The girls were getting along remarkably well. Things were going so well we decided to go shopping. Kyeong Sook had some knowledge of the bus system, and when her judgment was a bit off, we found many people willing to lend advice, since a great many in Seoul spoke English. I still feared getting lost, and faith, like a rope tied from the house to the barn in a blizzard, guided me.

Most of the time I felt like an ambassador representing American mothers of adopted Korean children. Everywhere we went people kept staring at us. I was extremely glad I was dressed up. Being a lover of casual clothes, I'd packed one dressy outfit just in case. I was glad I had decided to wear it that day. We were in Youido, which is the Manhattan of Seoul, and everyone took the dressy approach. For the most part the people were quite stylish, with men in dark suits and ties. Women wore pantsuits or skirts with jackets. I was not wearing any make-up, and it was a big mistake. For women under the age of sixty, the natural look was not acceptable. Younger women did not have enough status to go barefaced in public.

Although it was May and quite warm, all the young girls wore thick white tights. Well-dressed women kept casting sidelong glances at my daughter's above-the-knee dresses, anklet socks and bare legs, so I knew we were committing some kind of cultural fashion error.

We arranged to meet the assistant director of the orphanage where we were staying at 3:00 o'clock. He was going to give us a ride back to the orphanage. Even though I'd had much contact with him over the week, he was so formal it was impossible to get to know him. Still he was kind and cheerful, and he wanted Kyeong Sook to understand that Seoul was a thriving, modern city and was much more like the United States than she realized.

My first male-female Korean cultural relationship lesson began. It turns out that there is no "ladies first" custom in Korea's traditions. Tradition, which many older people still adhere to, dictates that a man opens the door and enters first. The woman goes in after him. I didn't know this. Each time he opened the door I waltzed in first. Of course he also entered first and we kept slamming our bodies together. I was mortified. The fifth time he opened a door, it dawned on me to wait. I let him enter first. He smiled and gave me a nod of approval.

Each time I tried to walk by his side, he quickened his stride; it seemed he wanted me to walk a few paces behind him. Otherwise he was friendly and appeared to enjoy the afternoon with us.

When we got back to our room, I was exhausted and dirty feeling, and I wanted a hot shower. Cold water barely dribbled out of the hand-held shower nozzle. I hunched up my shoulders, and let the icy water trickle over me. Vanessa begged for hot water to wash up with, so I heated water in the teapot. She was thirsty too. It was 1989, and back then it was difficult to find bottled water in Korean grocery stores, so we constantly had to boil water for drinking. It took hours to cool. Most of the time we gave over to drinking it warm.

"Your feet and legs are filthy," I said to Kyeong Sook. "Go wash up."

"When I lived here I always looked like this," she answered. "After a while you just get used to it." She slipped into her now dirty-white tennis shoes with the heals mashed down and dashed off to the playground.

At dinnertime the orphanage cafeteria served us yet another bowl of soup, spicy and delicious, rice and *kimchi*. Since the orphanage kids were in school all day, the evening dinner break was Kyeong Sook and Vanessa's only opportunity to talk and play with their new friends. There was no language barrier. Vanessa spoke a handful of Korean words with the greatest of ease.


ON OUR LAST DAY IN KOREA the director invited us to a farewell dinner at his home. A table was pulled out, and the family sprawled on the floor; everybody sat loose-limbed, all but me. My legs were folded under me like the roots of an old bent apple tree. Yet, like the others, I was content in the peace of the moment. I could almost see into a summer of my childhood. If only in my mind I was again at the kitchen table in my great-grandma's house, gathered with the deep-eyed uncles, and aunties with their high-cheeked faces. It didn't matter that the conversations on this day were taking place in the Korean, I could feel the power of togetherness, and it needed no translation.

Kyeong Sook had not yet said that she was planning to go back to the United States with me, but I could tell she wanted to, and I knew better than to ask her again. Her little blue suitcase was already packed, and she had begun to loop her arm around me when we walked, not in a cuddly way, as was the custom for Korean females to walk together. It was more like she'd anchored herself to me and was hanging on.

Our flight home left at 10:00 o'clock in the morning. Vanessa woke up at dawn to call Gary.

"How about if I make a batch of chocolate chip cookies for you to eat when you get home tomorrow.," he suggested.

"Daddy, it's already tomorrow here." Vanessa giggled, then she handed the phone to me.

"Pick up some calamine lotion," I requested over thousands of miles of telephone line. "Kyeong Sook has been complaining about mosquito bites."

I exhaled deeply. "Yep—Kyeong Sook is coming home with us."


I PACKED, AND VANESSA CHOSE an outfit to wear on the airplane. She picked her new yellow sweat suit, comfortable clothes for a long flight. I bid goodbye to the director, and I left the donation money with him, including the thick wad of Korean won I had left in my purse.

We walked over to the main building so Vanessa and Kyeong Sook could say goodbye to their friends. It was now mid-May, and I noticed the orphanage girls were no longer wearing the thick white tights. Now each girl was wearing white anklet socks. It meant spring had officially arrived.

We climbed into the taxi to go to the airport. Everyone had been so kind to us I was overwhelmed with emotion. I looked at Kyeong Sook. She averted her eyes. There were still so many questions. How would an adoptive mother with a need to feel trusted and an almost twelve-year-old with a lot of anger and hurt ever begin to get to know one another? How would my relationship with Vanessa change? And what about Jay. What kind of an impact was all of this having on him?

We were leaving Korea, and my heart tipped away. I stared out the window. The sky opened into high gray overcast; we passed through the outskirts of the city where wild flowers covered the hillsides. Rich green rice fields streamed by and a rainbow arched wide over the hills.

WE BOARDED THE AIRPLANE and buckled our seat belts. Kyeong Sook fell asleep. Vanessa watched the movie, and I curled up and read my book. Kyeong Sook woke up and she didn't look good at all.

"My head is hurting and I'm hot," she said. Little blisters had formed all over her face. There were more spots on her neck and arms.

"Good grief, you've got chicken pox."

There wasn't anything else I could do, so for the entire flight back to the US I sponged her with a damp washcloth and smoothed her black hair.

# ⇒ WINTER OF FAITH, 1989 ⇐

We knew the trip back to Korea must have had a profound effect on Kyeong Sook. Yet there wasn't an immediate change in her demeanor. Even though I knew it was completely unrealistic, a part of me wished that our homecoming would have had a sudden drastic effect, like in the movie the *Wizard of Oz,* when Dorothy opened the door and walked from Kansas to Oz, and everything went from black and white to brilliant color.

Instead when we got home Kyeong Sook was as sullen as before. At times she was even more somber because going back to Korea had opened up old wounds. She had calmed down now that she no longer felt forced into being adopted. She had made the choice to join our family, and this much she admitted. It was clear she also felt defeated.

I look back at this as the true beginning of her grieving process. She had let go of Korea and was mourning her loss.

I was the one who returned from Korea reflecting an immediate change. I was a more compassionate mother. Being in Korea allowed me to glimpse things from Kyeong Sook's point of view. I had more tolerance for her surly moods. I understood the cultural changes she was up against. Staying at the orphanage gave me a chance to think about what it might be like for Vanessa or Jay if they were suddenly taken from me, and were adopted into another family, in another part of the world.

After experiencing Korea, I realized that adopting Korean children defined the identity of our family far more than I ever could have imagined it would. Gary also had begun to have inklings of the enormity of what we had done.

Korean children had been adopted into our family. Common sense told us that as a mixed-race family it was necessary for us to somehow put down roots in the Korean community. My basic philosophy holds tight: culture and heritage are important, not just for American Indian children, but for all children. Since two of our kids were of Korean descent it made us "in-laws" in the Korean way. As their parents we believed we were responsible for leading our children to people who could teach them something of Korean ways and beliefs, and Gary, Vanessa and I needed to be brought into Korean culture as well.

THE FIRST CHANGE WE MADE in the winter of 1989 was to begin attending an all-Korean church. We were not an every-Sunday-church-going family. Sometimes Sunday mornings found us in the Lord's mountain house or camping on his beachfront property. Still the Korean church made a huge effort to include us. There was no time to wonder if we would be accepted. Reverend Lee and the other church members extended their kindness to our family time after time.

We allowed ourselves to be treated as guests for the first month, and then we knew it was time to offer to help out with the work that needs doing within a church community. I volunteered to help with the woman's group rummage sale, and Gary offered to drive his truck to pick up loads of donated items. Pitching together in a team effort builds sturdy bonds. It wasn't long before I felt myself part of the group of woman. I felt accepted.

I'm a light-skinned mixed-blood, and everyone else was one hundred percent Korean with black-brown eyes and very dark hair. Their appearance, strangely enough, reminded me of my childhood family, of my Indian great-grandparents and the black-haired second cousins I so little resemble.

Even though it was clear the Korean community welcomed us, I felt uncomfortable. In Korea, I was definitely a foreigner first, then an American, but in the Korean American community my new friends made it clear they viewed me as only Caucasian. They just assumed I led a typical white lifestyle with cultural traits and thought patterns similar to other Caucasian people they knew.

"I'm also American Indian," I told them, and I watched their faces go blank.

"You don't look like an Indian." One of the women said.

I could feel a certain set to my jaw as they all scrutinized me, looking for signs. I have what my grandfather wished he'd had, I don't bear the stereotypical physical signs of looking Indian. I knew the next question. I knew she was going to ask how much? How much Indian am I?

My smaller than average eyes struggled in order to see over the tops of my cheekbones. I sifted through my beliefs, and searched for a way to tell them that underneath my light brown hair and green eyes, I'm a genuine Cherokee, Delaware, Seneca Indian, a one hundred percent mixed-blood. And that being an Indian person was granted to me through a long line of ancestors. It rose from a feeling planted deep inside me, that oriented my whole sense of being, and dominated how I viewed the world and lived my life, and was not based on whether or not I had stone black eyes and straight black hair.

Soon I discovered the element of Korean culture I love best, Korean picnics. An armload of *bulgogi* covered the grill, and a circle of friends surrounded the barbecue. Everyone had a pair of chopsticks in hand and turned slices of sizzling beef. A picnic table was laden with platters of *mandu, dat dok*, and bowls of *chap chae*. We could always count on romaine lettuce leaves with red bean sauce for dipping, and three rice cookers stood ready in a row.

There was laughter around the table. After another helping of dry cuttle fish, after we ate as much food as we could hold, we would find a grassy spot under a shade tree, pull out a folk guitar, stretch back on the grass, and sing. The familiar melody always had me humming along, while the group sang the lyrics in Korean. We rested just long enough for our food to settle, and then it was time to play games.

There were sack races, three-legged races, or we would hold hands, circling around with more singing. Everyone played, and everyone sang, the grandmas and grandpas, even babies were encouraged to join in, and there is always someone willing to lend a helping hand. I found it wildly wonderful that fancy equipment was never needed for game playing. We had a ball, a blindfold, two gunnysacks and we had each other. Just people enjoying one another was not always an easy thing to find. These gatherings left me with a contented feeling, a sense of belonging, like I had when I went to a family reunion.

However, our new group of Korean friends hadn't felt like family in the beginning. Gary and I needed to have faith, because in giving our children this opportunity, we also had to let go of them in order to allow them to be absorbed and find their place within the Korean community. Our new friends were equally willing to absorb Vanessa too, and she flowed within the group as the only non-Asian kid.

I've heard adoptive parents say they want the Korean American community to accept their family on the adoptive parents' terms and not to absorb their kids. They don't want them to take over. We didn't feel this way. I wanted my kids to have the same opportunity to be immersed in the Korean community as they did within the Native American community. The difference was Korean culture was unfamiliar. We were making new friends and allowing them to take our children into a world unknown to us.

While Jay, age six, and Kyeong Sook, age twelve, explored the constantly evolving questions of what it meant to be Korean American, Gary and I sank in roots and worked to build lasting relationships and to let our new friends know that our interest in doing so was heartfelt.

Our church group took turns hosting small gatherings at each other's homes. Although shyness gripped me, still I offered to hold a party at our house. Sometimes the women's group gathered in my kitchen. Once I got over my fear of the unknown, it felt great to be part of the group and pulling my weight.

The children began attending Korean language classes. The language school was a new addition to the church program, and since very few of the Korean American kids at the church spoke Korean, our children fit right in. The classes were casual, and moved at a slow pace. Gary and I were invited to join in, and there were only three of us in the adult class; Gary, another Caucasian man, and me. We worked from the same beginning language books our kids used.

JAY'S SKILL WITH KOREAN language progressed at a fast rate, yet he didn't want to be friends with any of the Korean kids from church. Jay slammed down his toothbrush. "Why do we have to go to church with all those Koreans?"

"Has it ever occurred to you that you are one of those Korean people too?" Vanessa said. "It's worse for me, I'm the only kid in the whole Sunday school who isn't Korean." Vanessa rolled her eyes. "No one seems to understand, I don't like going because I feel so different."

"Yes, I do understand." Kyeong Sook replied. "That's how I feel all the time."

Jay leaned against the bathroom sink listening to Vanessa and Kyeong Sook talk, and he stared into the mirror. Instead of reflecting light, his eyes were brownout; he made no sound, no movement.

Sometimes we got a babysitter and let Jay and Vanessa stay home while we went to church and other Korean community events. Only it wasn't long before they both discovered that the children at our new church were no different from any of their other friends. Soon they became part of the gang of shrieking, laughing kids.

"Edwin was in Sunday school this morning." Vanessa said.

"Who?" I asked.

"Edwin. He's Korean mom, and he's in my class at school." Vanessa tilted her head to one side and said, "He sure was surprised to see me at church."

"I know," Jay chimed in, "his brother is in my class."

It wasn't long before Kyeong Sook discovered that a girl in her Sunday school class also attended their school. The girl was a grade ahead of Kyeong Sook.

Over a period of many months, I watched Kyeong Sook make a gradual change. She began to make friends at school. Prior to going to Korea, she found fault with every American girl she met, even girls who were Korean American. Now, even though she continued to be highly critical, she was beginning to give other kids a chance to become her friends. Soon after, she stopped insisting that life in Korea was better than life in the United States. She began to tell me about the various ways Korea and America were different, and how each had special qualities of their own.

Our social life became more active than ever before. One friendship within the Korean community led to another. We did a lot of to-ing and fro-ing. My new friend, Jung Hee, invited our family to attend her sister's lavish, traditional-style, Korean wedding. A few weeks later we went to a very large, jolly, sixtieth birthday party for Reverend Lee's wife, held at a swank restaurant. Or sometimes we gathered at the homes of our new Korean community friends, and played board games and talked over bowls of *naengmyon* noodles. Later we sat in front of the fireplace, and our kids toasted marshmallows for dessert.

It was fairly common for us to spend one Saturday night with our Korean community friends, and the next Saturday night hanging out with the group of white adoptive parents we were friends with, who all had children adopted from Korea. I had hoped to someday bring these two groups of friends together, so that we didn't have to live such a divided lifestyle.

Hanging out with an all-Asian group allowed me to glimpse a whole other side of what it feels like to be Korean American in the United States. I felt myself shrink when strangers on the street muttered rude comments about Orientals. That word. *Oriental.*

Uncomfortable situations popped up regularly. Like the day we were swimming with our Asian friends in a hotel pool. As soon as our children jumped into the water, a white family scooped their kids out of the pool. When we brought our children in for lunch, the other family climbed back into the swimming pool. To prove it wasn't my imagination I managed to move our kids in and out of the water all day. Each time our sweet, kind-eyed children swam, these parents pulled their kids out, as if our children's brown-skinned bodies might somehow pollute the water.

Or we found ourselves ignored in restaurants. Table after table of people would be served water and menus, and then their meals came. The waitress looked right through us. When we strolled through the gift shop, the proprietor, unaware that two teenaged Asian boys were with Gary and me followed them around the store. Gary leaned forward, expecting the man to apologize for treating the boys like shoplifting suspects. Instead the man glared at us, and refused to help find what we were looking for, and turned his back abruptly. These are examples, not one-time occurrences, and this kind of thing happened far too often. It left me saddened, but not shocked. It was the reason my paternal grandfather tried to live as invisible as possible, hoping he would be able to escape facing racism.

When I was ten I remember my grandfather lifting up my chin with his rough brown hand, and he said, "Usually it's better not to claim you're Indian." My grandfather never talked about his life in the Indian Territory. For those stories I had to go to my great-aunt Lydia, my grandfather's sister. My grandfather never spoke about growing up in Oklahoma; instead his stories began when he moved to California, got his first job, married, bought a house and raised my dad. My grandfather came to California in 1929; he was nineteen years old with only an eighth grade education. Without money he had no choice and rode in train boxcars. He saw the move to California as a new beginning, a chance to leave being Indian behind him. Far from claiming an Indian identity, he ignored it as if it might eventually go away.

In time my great-grandparents also moved to California, and when my dad was a kid they lived in a circus tent. By the time I was born in 1953, my great-grandparents lived in a house. It was an old single-story white frame house, with a rock behind each door. The house was always filled with relatives. My great-grandma could prepare a meal to feed fifteen of us. I loved to sit beside her coal black stove, watching her roll out noodle dough, listening to her stories about sitting on the high porch, watching sunsets when she was a girl, and the way the shapes of the earth changed as the sun moved across the sky. She spoke of a time when Kansas and Oklahoma belonged to nature.

"When I was twelve, Terry Lynn," my great-grandma once told me, "I could hitch up the team and drive the wagon to town by myself. Back then the prairie was covered with grass that rippled and changed color when the wind blew on it." I loved to listen. My great-grandma's words allowed me to glimpse pictures of a world unknown to me.

My great-grandpa's stories came silently, like clouds floating in the sky. We sat together and smelled the rain, and there was the time he spotted two raccoons high in a pine tree. For occasional treats my great-grandpa took me into town for bubble gum or an ice cream cone. He went out of his way to meet up with folks and tell them I was his great-granddaughter. I was a golden-brown-haired child with eyes that hinted of mountain sage. My great-grandparent's Cherokee skin and black hair was not passed on to me; to me they handed down stories.

The old ways were important to my great-Uncle Will, my grandfather's eldest brother and I longed to know what he knew. I admired Uncle Will in a ten-year-old way that made me wish he'd take me with him to those places he went dressed in beadwork and deer-skin leggings. But my grandfather shot angry arrows out of his eyes, so I knew I was not supposed to want it.

After Sunday dinner sometimes I walked with my five cousins the half-mile to town to buy penny candy. My older cousins all had dark brown hair and skin much darker than mine. Once a man came out of the store, grabbed my cousin Ronny by the arm and said, "I want you Indian kids to get on out of here." In spite of the awful moment somewhere down deep inside I felt delighted, he'd called us "Indian kids."

I knew that my grandfather and my Uncle Will were practically full Indian, and I didn't understand why my grandfather didn't want me to be Indian too. I figured it had something to do with my light brown hair, my freckled skin, and about the way everybody always said, "Geez, you look white just like your mom."

The year I turned twelve my great-grandpa died and my great-grandma went to live in a house trailer behind my Uncle Will's house. All of a sudden everything changed; our big Sunday family dinners at great-grandma's came to an end. Without my great-grandparents around, I was cut off from any kind of an Indian identity. Sometimes when I felt brave I told the kids at school we were Cherokee. But there was always someone who would say, "You don't look Indian. You're probably just making it up."

Eventually, I began tucking the fact that I was Indian deep inside me, and I didn't tell anyone. Then in my late teens I had my first opportunity to fill out one of those forms that asks you to mark your ethnic status. It said to check only one box. My dad was with me at the time.

"Take your time," he said. "This is probably the most important decision you will ever make."

I chose the box labeled American Indian, refusing to follow my grandfather's path of passing. Though I would not fully understand what this meant until becoming pregnant at nineteen with a baby that wasn't white.

By now my grandfather lived in Oregon, and we seldom spoke on the phone. Once a year he came to visit me, and there would be a lot of tension in the air and little emotion in our relationship; I put up with him, more or less until the year he turned eighty-two, when his negative feelings about being Indian began to ease off.

We sat on the couch, side by side, and my grandfather's ankles were thin inside brown wool slippers. His voice was low, barely above a whisper, and for the first time he told me what it was like for him to be an Indian boy growing up in Oklahoma. In that moment I saw the world through his eyes, lived his life, and felt his emotions. He told me about a sign near his childhood home which read, "White Man Don't Let The Sun Go Down," and it meant that if you were white, then you'd better leave by dark. There was a sparkle in my grandfather's eyes,

TERRA TREVOR

"Back then we could follow a sun set for miles and not meet up with anybody."

At the time I'd just returned from a visit to Oklahoma, and I rattled off questions, feeling like a ten-year-old kid again, and this time that deep empty space inside me began to fill up.

The next day I went to my Uncle Will. Long gray hair feathered behind his ears, and he peered at me over the rims of his glasses. His cheekbones seemed to have gradually risen higher over the years and formed small mountains below his eyes.

I opened an aluminum-folding chair and sat down. "When I was little I remembered crossing the Mississippi." I confided that day to my uncle. "But now all I can remember is the wagons and the tall grass." I watched my uncle's face, searching for his thoughts. "My mom said it must have been a dream because nobody had wagons when I was growing up in the 1950s and we lived in California."

Uncle Will struck a match and lit the lantern. Our night shadows danced against the smooth silver wall of his trailer house. I saw my reflection in the window, the profile of my nose, and the way my cheekbones jutted out and formed little mountains below my eyes, curving gently to my jaw line. Uncle Will raised his head, "You are a hundred percent Indian. You know that don't you? I can see it in you," he said.

I knew Uncle Will was not talking about the way I looked on the outside. He'd found an opening into a deep space inside me, the special part of me that didn't know my outside was covered up with white skin.

Uncle Will closed his eyes and said, "There is a kind of power that is sent for telling the stories." His eyes stayed closed and I thought his mind had probably gone to where those at center drum go, when they are drumming and singing. It's a place I can't find. Yet when I write stories about the time when short buffalo grass and red dirt covered the Great Plains between Kansas and the Red River, I know I'm getting close.

I don't have any pictures of my dad's side of the family. The film was overexposed the day we took the photograph where all of the relatives lined up according to our generation. In the photo my great-aunts and uncles were grouped together. These are my grandfather's brothers and sisters and the line didn't hold a white face. The next group was my dad and his sister and cousins, the first half-blood generation in the family.

Being half Indian gave eyes of hazel, wavy or straight brown hair. My brother and sister and I stood with the largest group of cousins. We are more genetically mixed than our parents. On the outside, only our tiny deep-set eyes and high-cheeked faces told of our ancestral past. Yet soon enough we would become the elders.

Growing up in my family I observed a lot of denial of being Indian. At times I felt part of me was missing, and the part of my heritage denied became more important than the part of me that was clearly defined. This was the main reason I decided it was important for Jay and Kyeong Sook to grow up with the opportunity to be surrounded with Koreans and Korean Americans. They could reject an Asian identity if they wanted, but I wanted them to feel at home with what they were rejecting. It is key in choosing, and pivotal for mixed race people. I wondered if being a Korean adoptee in some ways might be similar to being mixed race.

The strong connection I felt to my own origins helped me understand why some adoptive parents might choose not to embrace their adopted children's race and the ethnic culture from their land of birth. In transracial adoption an underlying concern emerges that biological families never have to face: our children's history and race is not the same as ours.

Since Jay and Kyeong Sook had been adopted without a documented paper trail, I seldom spoke about my own well-documented family heritage. I discovered my silence made Jay uncomfortable. When I finally opened the subject up, he relaxed and began to understand it was all right to express his feelings about not knowing who his birth family was.

Jay put his hand on my arm. "Mom, I just hope someday I can meet my birthmother and my birthfather."

I nodded. "I hope someday you can too." I ran my hand through his hair, pushing the bangs off his forehead.

We didn't have any information on Jay's family in Korea. Even though he was only six-years-old, it was clear from our conversation that he had spent a great deal of time trying to imagine what they might be like.

This conversation paved the way for Jay to begin sharing intimate feelings more often. A few nights later when Gary was tucking Jay into bed, Jay admitted that the number one reason he had decided against joining a recently formed Cub Scout troop was because he didn't feel comfortable. Jay was not a shy boy. It was unusual for him to make this sort of comment. Gary had noticed that something didn't feel quite right at the meetings. This particular all-white troop was cliquish and not very friendly towards them. Something about the experience had felt peculiar to Gary, but he wasn't sure what it was. For some reason, some of the other fathers deliberately excluded Jay. Being an extremely good child who always followed the rules and obeyed orders, Jay was puzzled. Gary was puzzled too. He had talked about it briefly with Jay, but Jay wanted to shrug the whole thing off. Not knowing what else to do, Gary shrugged it off too.

I thought back to my college days, 1972, a time when most of my friends were American Indian. When we were traveling from Arizona to California and needed to get a motel room, it was my job to sign the register, and my girlfriends would join me in the room later.

"It's better if you do it," my friends always said. "They won't hassle you."

I felt awful about needing to sneak in order to avoid having my friends being treated poorly, and I hated the fact that since I looked white I was designated to do the bidding.

My best friend Marie, who had a sexy figure, and huge dimples, was Hopi Indian.

Oftentimes I watched Caucasian men treat Marie disrespectfully. When the same men came on to me disrespectfully, and I told them no, they listened. Yet they acted as if Marie had no right to say no, as if she had no rights at all.

When I was with Marie, in her neighborhood, where the streets were unpaved, and only dark-skinned people were welcome, it was necessary for me to hide my long, light brown hair under the hood of my sweatshirt. It didn't matter that I was a mixed blood; I was still too white to be accepted. It didn't matter that Marie was a kind, wonderful, person. She was not accepted in many white social circles just because she was Indian.

My chest tightened knowing that strangers would always look at Jay and Kyeong Sook and only see Asian. They would wonder if they spoke English with an accent, or if they spoke English at all. They would never be the recipients of white privileges. The term *yellow fever* took on new meaning when I realized there would be those men who would see Kyeong Sook as *Oriental* and *exotic*, and that she would be subject to the same type of treatment my friend Marie had to put up with.

There are some people in America who believe that racism is less of a problem now than it used to be. Though anyone who isn't white knows that this is not true.

One Sunday morning, about eight months after we began attending the Korean church, Gary turned to me and said, "I've been doing some thinking. As a white father of an Asian son and daughter it has been really difficult coming to terms with the societal privileges I have."

"Yes," I said. I stepped toward him and slid onto the seat beside him.

Gary sighed. "I'm aghast at how Asian people are often treated." Gary looked at me and crossed his arms. "Today at the mall when Kyeong Sook was standing in line to pay for some earrings there was an Asian women standing in line behind her. The clerk looked right through them. They had to wait much longer than the others, and kept getting pushed to the back of the line."

We stared at each other for a few seconds. Then Gary took a deep breath, and said, "Being raised in a white family, in a white middle class community has put me at a terrible disadvantage. I've never experienced what our kids go through." He paused, took off his glasses and pinched the bridge of his nose. "The ability to move through life and not experience racial profiling never occurred to me until I saw it happen to my kids."

That winter Gary interviewed for a new job and was immediately considered for the position. Then the interviewer admitted a highly qualified applicant, a Korean man, interviewed for the same position earlier in the day and his resume had been tossed into the trash after he left. Gary turned to the man who had interviewed him and said, "Two of my kids are adopted from Korea, and I can't work for you."

The director of the orphanage in Korea where we stayed telephoned. "Can you do a favor for me?" he asked. He wanted to know if we would host a Korean woman who was a social worker. She wanted to stay with an American family and would bring her ten-year-old daughter. The daughter didn't speak any English, and it would be their first time in the United States.

At the airport we met a dark-haired, dark-eyed woman about my age, exactly my height, and a light-brown-haired girl with a grin that stretched from ear to ear. The little girl said something to her mother in a language that wasn't Korean. The woman introduced herself as Ahryun. There was a twinkle in her eye,

"We're speaking Swedish, my daughter Tanna is half Swedish."

The part of me that isn't Indian and German is Swedish from my mom's side of the family. Only I'm the great-granddaughter of Swedish immigrants who migrated to Colorado, and my mom was steeped in western, rocky mountain culture.

Nine-year-old Vanessa and ten-year-old Tanna hit it off immediately. From the start Ahryun and I were like high school girl-friends reunited. With our bare feet poking into blue morning glories we sat on the backyard grass squeezing juice from lemons to make lemonade.

Ahryun tossed a handful of hollowed out rinds into the compost pit. She was a social worker in Korea and placed Korean adoptees in Sweden. She was married to a Swedish man, and they had two daughters. Tanna and her younger sister (who was in Korea with her father) were born and had been raised in Korea. The family was bicultural, they spoke fluent Korean and Swedish, and divided their time between Korea and Sweden. But in the fall they planned to move permanently to Sweden.

"My husband is a language instructor at Han Gook University." Ahryun bit at the edge of a lemon rind, and then she asked, "Do you know what *han gook* means?"

"Yeah." I replied. "It means Korean."

She giggled. "But do you know what it means in Swedish? In Swedish the word *han gook* means penis. Can you imagine the jokes people make when they hear that my husband teaches at Han Gook University?"

For lunch I served sandwiches with tortilla chips and my home-made salsa.

"Did you say salsa?" Ahryun's eyes were wide. "In Korea a word that sounds like "salsa" means diarrhea." We doubled over laughing, the kids gagged. We made it into a game and found dozens of words with dual meanings.

Jay fell into the habit of climbing into Ahryun's lap and cuddling with her. He was small for his age, and he folded himself onto her back, and she carried him around the house and out in the yard. I looked at Jay's face; his facial features and the color of his skin were almost exactly like hers. Of course, I thought: this is how Jay would look with his birthmother. A part of me was jealous that Jay always wanted to be with her. It was my next big step in allowing

Jay to grow wings. After all, being Asian was his experience, not mine. I could best help him if I didn't get too involved in his personal search. My job was to help him put down roots, love him and provide a firm foundation he could build on. His formative years were like the layers of a cake. If the first layer was crumbly it would be harder to add the second layer in adolescence. Yet watching Jay cozy up to another mother, one who was Korean, tugged at my heart. It was another reminder of the enormous responsibility we'd undertaken by adopting Korean children.

It didn't take long for me to discover the joys of having two mothers caring for four children. It was wonderful having another mother around. From the first night on, we did dishes together, and we laughed and chatted as we worked along.

Usually I cooked dinner every day. Most of the time I fixed one-dish meals. Stacked enchiladas, hearty vegetable soups, or heaping bowls of pinto beans piled high with diced tomatoes, green chilies, and cilantro were typical fare. My secret to getting children to love bean dishes was to let them grate mounds of cheese and layer it with the beans.

Even on oh-so exhausting evenings, surprisingly, I could manage to get a pan of corn bread into the oven. My endurance had worn thin when it came to planning meals, making grocery lists, and shopping for food. All of those things I did and redid week after week. Still, cooking, even when I was weary, carried decided advantages over going out to dinner or making do with take-out food. Restaurants were best saved for when a burst of desire caught hold. I left passion to rule our plans for a dinner out, not weariness. If we ate dinner out too often the magic went away.

To be accurate our kitchen already had two cooks. Gary took up the holiday challenge. Barely sleeping at all he rose at dawn to get a turkey into the oven, and on a monthly basis he baked pies and scones. He mashed potatoes and made perfect gravy. Cooking the old-fashioned Irish way ran in his blood. He also worked along side me on the evenings when I fixed Korean food.

Yet I was the one who responded to the task of getting an ordinary dinner on the table night after night. When luck held there were leftovers. A portion of Monday's enchiladas was frozen for dinner on Friday. Tuesday's vegetable soup would be reheated again on Thursday. Except on Wednesday I couldn't figure out what to serve with the pan of corn bread. I winged it on Saturdays when a craving for pizza might take hold. Or sometimes on Saturdays Gary cooked. At any rate, just in case, I kept dinner flexible on Saturdays. Yet, before I caught my breath Monday arrived and it was time to start cooking dinners all over again. I was lucky because Gary was always happy with whatever I fixed. As long as I prepared it and set the table, he would eat gleefully, and usually he complimented me on what I served.

Our days with Ahryun and Tanna kept me much busier than average. Day after day dinner time caught me off guard, in the middle of doing something else, without a plan for dinner. At the end of the first week the grocery shopping needed to be done. I could tell Ahryun no longer wanted to be treated like company. We set off to do the marketing together with four children in tow. Tanna and Ahryun were amazed at the aisles of food. They had never seen anything like it. We loaded our cart, and I let the kids pick out special treats. Even though Ahryun and Tanna lived in Seoul, the family spent long stretches of time in Sweden. They were familiar with many western foods, but this grocery store was bigger and more overwhelming than anything they'd ever seen. From the way Ahryun described it, the small town near Stockholm where her husband's parent's lived, sounded similar to the small town in Ireland where Gary's father was from. I'd grocery shopped in Ireland, so I knew there were less food items available, and not as many brands to pick from. It made shopping less complicated and more tranquil. Gary's cousin from Ireland had been equally shocked his first time in a typical American Supermarket.

On the way home from the store I decided to stop by the Korean market. Ahryun's eyes lit up. "I miss eating Korean breakfast," she admitted.

The items she bought were new to me. I discovered there were two kinds of soy sauce. Besides the regular dark soy sauce, there was also a clear soup soy sauce. It's called "soup soy sauce" because it is used mostly for making soup.

"Sometimes I make *cho kanjang*, vinegar soy sauce." Ahryun instructed, "By adding two teaspoons of vinegar and a half-teaspoon of sugar and mixing it with two tablespoons of regular soy sauce."

I had stocked our refrigerator with *kimchi*, bean paste, plenty of fixings for making *chop chae*, and we had a twenty-pound sack of rice. Yet to a person who usually ate Korean food three times a day, our cupboards must have seemed bare.

That night for dinner, garden green beans became Sesame Green Beans when Ahryun cut the stems off of 2-lbs of green beans, and added:

*3 tablespoons of sesame oil*

*1 tablespoon of rice vinegar*

*1 tablespoon lemon juice*

*1 teaspoon fresh grated ginger*

*2 tablespoons sesame seeds*

She brought a large pot of water to boil, added the green beans and cooked them uncovered until they were crisp-tender. Next she drained them and set them aside. In a large bowl she whisked together the sesame oil, rice vinegar, lemon juice, grated ginger and sesame seeds until well blended, and then she added the green beans and tossed them in the sauce mixture until they were well coated.

The new fragrances in our kitchen brought out a light-hearted side of Kyeong Sook's personality. Her eyes were shining, dark hair rippled over her shoulders, and her face looked like it wanted to smile. She was cheerful and fun to be around.

Dried seaweed, I learned, needed to soak in a bowl of water. After a few hours it became sleek and slippery, perfect for soup.

A light went on inside Kyeong Sook. "This is the same kind of soup I always ate. It's my favorite soup," she said.

It turned out this seaweed soup was equal to what a peanut butter sandwich is for an American kid. Kyeong Sook had seconds, while Vanessa and Jay opted for peanut butter and jelly. Tanna wanted peanut butter and jelly too, because she wanted to do everything Vanessa did.

## Seaweed Soup *Miyok kuk*

*2 cups soaked and drained seaweed* (miyok)

*3 cups soup stock or water*

*2 tablespoons chopped garlic*

*1-tablespoon sesame oil*

*1-teaspoon soup soy sauce* (kuk kanjang)

Pour sesame oil in a deep skillet and stir-fry miyok with garlic, sesame oil, soup soy sauce and salt. When the miyok begins to sizzle, add 1 cup of soup stock. Repeat the process until you have added all 3 cups of water or soup stock. Bring to a boil and then lower the heat and simmer for a few minutes.

The second bowl of seaweed soup was also a point of discovery for Kyeong Sook. When she went to live in the orphanage at age ten, the price she paid was her memory. She realized she had become amnesic about her early years and had forgotten practically everything about her life before she went into the orphanage, and she couldn't remember much about her family in Korea. The one thing she did remember was that she didn't get along well with her Korean mother. The old days were similar to the new ones in that she wasn't getting along well with her American mother either. Most of the time she remained distant and was not about to allow any intimacy with anyone in her new so-called family. She was nearly thirteen, and already heavy into puberty, that age when the bedroom door slams shut. She spent every possible waking moment with her friends.

Kyeong Sook had accomplished one wonderfully important thing in the past year since returning from Korea. She had made lots of new friends. She was well liked by her school friends, and she even had a best friend. Although she was still often sullen or withdrawn at home, her teachers at school adored her. Other parents enjoyed having her around. To me this was a very good sign.

Vanessa was in heaven. With Tanna she felt she had gained the older sister friendship she was craving to have with Kyeong Sook. Vanessa and Jay had a comfortable sibling bond, and a close relationship. Vanessa began to mold her friendship with Tanna to resemble her relationship with Jay. There wasn't much language barrier. Vanessa taught Tanna English in exchange for Swedish language lessons.

HAVING TANNA SHARE A bedroom with Kyeong Sook and Vanessa allowed me to glimpse my daughters' relationship from a different perspective.

"Why Kyeong Sook not share?" Tanna demanded. It had become a new ongoing issue. Vanessa constantly wanted to use something that belonged to Kyeong Sook. Vanessa begged and Kyeong Sook said no. It was a tug of war that kept them in a perpetual state of being miffed. Patience worn, I told Vanessa to stop asking to borrow. Exhausted, I pleaded with Kyeong Sook to give in once in a while.

Through Tanna I learned Kyeong Sook often talked Vanessa into doing a favor for her by offering to let her borrow something. Then she figured out a way not to have to lend the item after all.

THE SATURDAY NIGHT MY grandparents, Meme and Pappa (my mother's parents) invited us to dinner, Ahryun said, "This food is the same as in Sweden." Then she said the whole house smelled like

Sweden. I didn't know what she meant. There wasn't any lutefisk, and the jam on our biscuits was boysenberry not lingonberry.

"I smell butter," she explained. "In Korea we do not use butter, and in Sweden everybody cooks with butter and puts butter on bread."

Now I understood. In Korea the whole country smelled like sesame and garlic. Only I had no idea butter carried a powerful aroma. I asked if our house smelled like butter too, and she said no. It was probably because we used margarine sparingly, if at all.

I looked around the dinner table. My mother was seated next to Gary, and they were dishing up potatoes, talking and laughing. My grandmother and Ahryun were engrossed in conversation. When my big happy family gathered with the aunts, uncles and cousins, we all talked at once just like we were doing now. Tanna's plate was heaping with a Jell-O salad made with tiny marshmallows, and she was giggling about something Kyeong Sook was saying. Jay was busy eating. My grandpa, Pappa, was telling Vanessa something while he cut up her meat.

Pappa's neck was tanned brown against white hair. His hair has been white for as long as I could remember. All my life Pappa has told me stories. He told stories of his boyhood in Colorado, about pretending different colored rocks were farm animals, about buying his first banjo and teaching himself how to play it. When he wasn't playing his banjo, Pappa enjoyed being in his backyard with the orange trees, plum trees, and tomato vines in summer. This was the only childhood home I'd ever known that hadn't gone away. Though I had lived with my mom and dad, my mother's parents (Meme and Pappa) were like second parents to me when my mom was sixteen, seventeen, and eighteen, and I was one, two and three.

My mom and my dad were good parents, as good as teenagers trying to grow up with a baby can be.

Ahryun helped my grandpa pick tomatoes. Tanna planted herself on a kitchen stool, and chatted with my grandmother. Each time Tanna spoke her eyebrows knitted together. She preferred to speak English, yet since she only knew a handful of words it reminded me of Kyeong Sook learning English at age ten. Tanna tried to become as Americanized as possible as soon as possible. In reality she was so European, that most of the time I forgot she was Korean.

Late that night when Tanna became angry with her mother, she snapped back in rapid fire Korean. The next thing I knew Ahryun began scolding Tanna in Swedish.

After the argument ended Ahryun explained, "In Korea it is not acceptable to argue with your parents, and the way Tanna spoke to me is forbidden in Korean culture. Yet she is an outspoken girl, and from living in Sweden she knows Swedish children, like American children, sometimes talk back to their parents."

There was a twinkle in Ahryun's eye, and she said, "My husband and I are more lenient than the average parents in Korea. Yet being a language teacher, my husband can not bear the way Tanna disgraces the Korean language when she talks back to me in Korean, so he insists she speak Swedish when she wants to argue with us."

Kyeong Sook listened wide-eyed. "I could argue as much as I wanted when I lived in Korea," she said. "Nobody cared what I did."

As ONE DAY FOLDED INTO THE next Vanessa, Jay and Tanna played together cheerfully for hours, constructing tents by draping sheets from the bunk beds. Or they spread a quilt outside under the trees and played make-believe games. I found doll dresses mixed with our laundry, and dirty socks and slightly worn T-shirts found their way to the bottom of the box where the dress-up play clothes were kept. I let go of my usual struggle to keep things tidy and enjoyed the messy house filled with happy children.

After I read the kids the *Tale of Tom Kitten,* they dressed our cat in doll clothes. Clementine, our calico cat, seemed to almost enjoy the attention. But then she leaped the four feet that separated my bedroom window from a neighbor's fence and disappeared wearing a lilac doll dress trimmed with eyelet. We imagined Mrs. Tabitha Twitchit saying, "Now keep your frock clean and walk on your hind legs." Our cat returned at nightfall. She must have trod upon her pinafore; there were several green smears.

Since Ahryun felt our washing machine was far too complicated to figure out, she added her laundry and Tanna's to our ever mounting hamper. On washdays she sorted the clothes, I loaded them into the machine, and when they came out of the dryer, we folded the laundry together.

Kyeong Sook began staying home more often and listened to the conversations Ahryun and I carried on while we did the housework.

Ahyrun pointed out my habit of dressing dowdy. "You're young and slim. You ought to wear shorts and tank tops." Long, loose dresses were the latest fashion rage. Though I often shopped for new clothes, more recently I'd slipped into a pattern of always purchasing and wearing the same similarly styled long baggy dresses. It felt wonderful to be inspired enough to search my closet and begin pairing summer outfits which made me look as good as I felt.

Tanna and Ahryun stayed with us most of the summer, and there was never a dull moment. We fixed dinner together, and while the food was in the oven, we sat outside sipping ice tea and watched the kids play in the yard. It was a season of endless ocean views, walking on sandy beaches, and rocky shores, and discovering tide pools. Gary felt like he'd won the lottery: I was always in a cheerful, relaxed mood when he came home from work.

Most evenings after dinner we all went for walks along the beach. Even though by this time of the day the sun was nearly setting, Tanna always wore her favorite lemon yellow sun hat.

"Why aren't we eating ice cream?" she asked. We laughed. I gave her thumbs up. Gary looked at me, "Yeah, why aren't we eating ice cream?" he asked.

We all trooped out to the pier, and Gary bought ice cream cones.

THE SUMMER NIGHTS WERE star-filled and warm.

"Can we sleep outside?" Vanessa begged.

"Can we? Please, Mom." Jay put his face next to mine and gave me a light kiss on the cheek.

Kyeong Sook tipped back her chair, balancing on the rear legs. "Can I invite a friend over?" she asked. I told her she could, and she called her best friend, Janelle. Then a few minutes later Kyeong Sook said, "Instead of staying here, Janelle wants to know if I can spend the night at her house?"

I told her she could, and fifteen minutes later when Janelle's mother honked the horn, Kyeong Sook ran out the front door with her overnight bag in her hand and a smile on her face.

Gary got out a large blue plastic tarp and spread it on the grass in the backyard. Vanessa found a queen sized quilt perfect to sleep on. There was an argument about who would get the sleeping bag that wasn't lumpy, and a discussion took place about how to divide two cans of root beer into three equal shares.

"I'm not sleeping in the middle," Tanna said.

"I will," Vanessa offered.

An ocean breeze swept through the propped open screen door, carrying the scent of jasmine, and I let out a deep sigh of contentment.

Each day wet bathing suits hung from our shower rod, and there were always at least six beach towels draped over the back fence. The floors in every room of the house were gritted with sand. It was the perfect summer and we treasured every moment of it.

## ⊰ WINTER, 1990 ⊱

My hopes were pretty high in the fall when the pastor of the Korean church called, saying he wanted to invite everyone in our community who had adopted Korean children to a Korean dinner.

"I'm also planning to open the language school to anyone with an interest and let the families with adopted Korean children know our Korean community supports them, and that we are willing to help bring a stronger Korean identity into their children's lives," Reverend Lee said.

Over a course of five years since adopting Jay, we'd made numerous close friendships with other families in our town that had also adopted children from Korea. All of our friends now embraced a multicultural awareness and made an attempt to weave Korean culture into their lives. I had been wanting to introduce my adoptive parent group friends, to my Korean community friends, and this would be the perfect opportunity. Reverend Lee planned to invite the entire Korean adoption support group in our town, which had grown considerably, so this dinner would include a few families that we barely knew.

Transracial adoption attitudes had begun to change. One of the few things you could always be sure about was that there would be changing views regarding transracial adoption. But with white parents of Asian adopted children there still was, and probably always will be, a divide of those who believed it was perfectly OK to raise their Asian children within an all-white society without frequent contact with other Asians. And there were those white adoptive parents who had begun to understand it was their responsibility to help their children develop an essential link to Asian identity.

I provided the addresses, and invitations went out to twenty families. I suspected about half of the group invited would send regrets. The other half, which included my close friends, I thought might want to attend, and I shared this information with Reverend Lee.

In Korean culture it is crucial to have more than enough food to offer guests. What is left over is packed up and sent home with family and friends.

Three days before the dinner Reverend Lee called me on the telephone.

"Has anyone contacted you? So far I've only heard from five of the families and four sent regrets."

I was stunned.

"Well, sometimes the idea of a church dinner puts people off," he offered. Reverend Lee was never one to push his religious preferences onto others. It was the quality I adored best about him; it was the reason I felt so comfortable attending his church.

"I guess I should have called everyone and explained that we aren't trying to convert them," he joked. I laughed, but it was a futile attempt to cover my embarrassment. I couldn't believe that fifteen families, many of them our close friends, had failed to respond to the R.S.V.P. I couldn't believe it. Our friends *knew* we attended the

Korean church. They would have recognized the name on the invitation. They knew from talking with me that most everyone in the Korean community, regardless of their particular brand of religion, banded together and attended Korean community events that were often held in the fellowship hall at this Korean church.

I knew the women of the church had been knocking themselves out. They were prepared to serve a meal fit for royalty. I suspected that some of the adoptive parents invited were unable to attend because they simply had other plans, and just didn't realize they needed to respond to the invitation.

On the day of the big dinner our family arrived early. The Korean Consul General introduced himself to me. He bowed and shook my hand. His wife and children were with him. Many other special guests were present, and a large banner announced the formal opening of the Korean language school.

The women in the church had prepared massive amounts of the best Korean foods. Craft tables and games were set up for the children. The banquet room was filled with people, all Korean American families, and we joined in the fun, but only one other adoptive family attended.

All afternoon Korean families came and went. Some dropped by for an hour or two, had lunch and visited with friends. Some of us stayed all day. I helped with serving. Gary was in charge of emptying the garbage can in the kitchen. Every few minutes he put a foot inside the can and smashed down the overflow of paper plates. When the can was full, he pulled out the bulging green plastic sack of trash, and stacked it outside. Kyeong Sook was a big help at the arts and craft table, assisting the younger kids. Vanessa spent much of the afternoon on the playground with a group of girls.

The barbecue was kept lit for hours, producing many platters of *bulgogi*. It was Jay's favorite treat, and there was enough of it for him to have as much as he wanted. Throughout the day everyone held on to the hope maybe more adoptive families might decide to drop by, yet none came.

That evening, when the sunlight changed from rosy to lavender, I sat in the church kitchen sipping iced barley tea, gossiping with the women. No one made any mention of the fifteen families who had failed to R.S.V.P, but since we live in a somewhat small town, the chilling facts were hard to overlook.

Later, Reverend Lee sat down beside me. The sun had set and the room was dim.

"Three days ago I called all of the adoptive families, introducing myself and encouraging them to come to the dinner." He said.

"You called all of them?"

He nodded. "I left quite a few voice mail messages, and no one called me back."

I frowned, and felt the blood rushing to my head. The shock of inviting twenty guests to dinner and then being ignored by fifteen of those invited must have felt like a slap in the face to Reverend Lee. It felt like a slap to me. Were my errant friends just clueless to social etiquette? Or did the name Eung Kyun Lee register in their minds as a person they could ignore and get away with it?

IT TURNED OUT THAT A NUMBER of our friends were sorry they had not joined in the Korean church dinner. So Gary and I devised a plan. That winter we invited our Korean church group, and all of our friends who had Korean children to celebrate Lunar New

Year with us. I pushed the coffee table out of the way and paced off the distance. "How many people do you suppose we can fit in the living room?"

Gary wrinkled his forehead. "If everyone comes it will be a tight squeeze. On the other hand if the weather is nice we can put up tables outside."

In Korea the major holiday of the winter months is Sol, the Lunar New Year. Shops close for several days, and families gather together and enjoy huge feasts of food and each other's company. The date of the holiday is based on the lunar rather than the solar calendar, so it changes every year. Usually it falls in January or February. Most people think of this as Chinese New Year, but Koreans observe this tradition as well.

One of the most treasured traditions of the New Year is getting new clothes. Even though most Koreans wear western-style clothing, traditional dress is still worn on Lunar New Year. The traditional *hanbok* for men and boys is made from shiny, colorful fabrics and consists of a short, loose shirt-jacket with long, full sleeves and wide, baggy trousers, which are tied at the ankle. Women or girls wear a *hanbok* with a very short, flared blouse crossed in the front, and a sash tied in a half bow and a long, high-waisted skirt in a bright contrasting color. Wearing a *hanbok,* children offer a New Year's bow before their parents and grandparents, honoring their elders.

Most Korean parents buy their children a *hanbok* and many adoptive parents of Korean children do the same. The kids jump at the chance to wear them. Most kids do, anyway; Jay said he didn't want one. However, when I came back from Korea with a red *hanbok* for Kyeong Sook, and a hot pink *hanbok* for Vanessa, both with shimmering rainbow sleeves, Jay said, "Do they make those for boys?"

I was able to order one for him through the mail, and it arrived in time for our big party.

Lunar New Year is part family reunion, part cultural revival. We had our guests remove their shoes at the door, which is a proper thing to do at a Korean party. Our friends filed in. Nearly everyone from our church came, and most of our adoptive family group friends attended too. The hall table was piled high with wrapped packages containing scented soaps and flavored coffees for that long-standing Korean tradition of giving a gift to each guest.

The scent of *kimchi*, garlic and sesame hung in the air like a spicy fog. I slid a baking sheet covered with dried seaweed out of the oven and with my fingers; quickly spread a film of sesame oil across the envelope-sized pieces. I salted each piece and folded it in half.

"You are supposed to spread the sesame oil on before you put it in the oven," my friend Jung Hee gasped. She popped a piece into her mouth. "Doesn't matter, it tastes good."

"The rice isn't cooking," I complained.

Two very old grandmothers with small wrinkled faces strained of the excess water and got the massive rice cooker I'd borrowed from the church to cook a perfect pot of rice.

I pulled a large pan filled with *chop chae* out of the oven.

"Is this all right?" The name *Chop chae* means various vegetables, and it is also made with transparent sweet potato-based spaghetti-like noodles, with small amounts of *bulgogi* mixed in. It was the first time I'd cooked Korean food for a large group of Koreans. I handed a pair of thin stainless steel chopsticks to one of the grandmothers. She tasted a bite, and nodded her head in approval.

It turned out the kind of *chop chae* I make is known in Korean circles as Chinese-style *Chop chae*.

*Duk kuk*, the special soup made with rice cakes, simmered on my stove. The clicking sound from the game Yut started up in the living room.

A guitar was pulled out. Everybody was encouraged to sing, and everyone was expected to play games. Our silliest game was the javelin. We wrote our names on wooden chopsticks, stood behind a line, and tossed them. Prizes, the sort you buy at the five-and-dime, were given out.


MY TWO GROUPS OF FRIENDS were not mixing and mingling as much as I'd hoped. All of the Korean families were busy playing games. Some of the Caucasian parents were wound up tighter than a ball of kite string and not eager to play. They stood around talking with each other. No one looked bored, yet they were not having as much fun as the group playing games.

Koreans, I'd discovered, like Indians, loved to gamble, so I opened with a lively jest of Fifty/Fifty. Everyone wanted in on the gambling. The tension broke and the group loosened up.

At ten-thirty at night the party was still going strong. Kyeong Sook swirled around the living room with a group of girls, her scarlet hanbok rippling. As Vanessa twirled her rainbow sleeves shimmered. Jay slid around the dining room in his stocking feet, wearing his brand new light pink hanbok, his face glowing, beaming with pride.

## ≈ SUMMER, 1991 ≈

The roses were in full bloom. Seven-year-old Jay had discovered the perks of riding his bicycle with the neighborhood boys. Gary and I had established a pattern of hour-long nightly walks. Sometimes after the kids went to bed, we sat outside on moonlit nights and drank a glass of wine, counting shooting stars while crickets and tree frogs serenaded us.

Kyeong Sook, now thirteen, seemed to be doing better, happy almost. Vanessa had recently turned ten. I was beginning to realize her adjustment from oldest to middle child was going smoother than I originally anticipated.

Summer was officially launched when I picked up the kids at noon on the last day of school. Jay stood outside his classroom and blinked back tears, "I just can't keep my balance. I keep falling down."

I called the doctor, and she told me to bring Jay in immediately. After a quick exam, Jay was sent to get an MRI (magnetic resonance imaging). There was a cancellation and our doctor wanted Jay to be seen right away.

The MRI, I was told, would take only about ten minutes. Casually the technician added, "If we see anything, we will give him an injection and run the scan again."

Jay's white tennis shoes were the only part of his body outside the tunnel-shaped piece of equipment. I stood quietly waiting for much longer than ten minutes. Someone came and gave Jay an injection and the scan was repeated.

As if in a dream I heard someone ask me to step into a consultation room. The scan showed a massive brain tumor. I tried to hang onto the information that not all tumors were malignant, but there was no way I could convince myself this tumor would be benign; it was spread out like a storm cloud.

"I want you both to go right over to the hospital," The radiologist said. Through my tears I looked at Jay's face, it was gray and blank. Without asking questions, without thinking, I gathered him up in my arms and rushed out the door, not towards the hospital. Instead I went to the park across the street.

The radiologist raced after me. "Where are you going?"

"Leave us alone for a while," I pleaded.

"Did you adopt him? he asked next. "Is he Vietnamese?"

"Korean," I corrected. I couldn't believe he asked me this. My son had just received a brain tumor diagnosis, and here I was answering a nosy adoption question. The radiologist pulled a tissue out of his pocket and handed it to me. I looked at Jay; his eyes were dark watery pools.

"Give us a few minutes alone," I said, turning my back. I picked up Jay, and carried him over to a patch of green grass. He leaned against my knees and the branches of an oak tree sheltered us.

"It means I have to have surgery again, doesn't it?" Jay's voice was low and throaty.

"Yes," I whispered. Wailing sobs shook through Jay's body. It was four o'clock on a Friday afternoon, the last day of school, a day that would normally have been filled with celebration. Instead our lives had just changed irrevocably.

I sat there holding him. I wasn't sure if I was going to throw-up or faint, yet I did neither. I sank into a deep, silent panic that made me feel calm. We sat in the park for a while, and then I carried Jay across the street to the hospital. He was admitted immediately.

"Well at least you have a television with a remote." I tried to hide the fear in my voice. Jay buttoned up his hospital pajamas; they were yellow with a red clown print. His serious eyes peered out at me. He looked healthy; it was impossible to understand something dangerous was growing deep inside his head.

"I'd better call your dad."

Jay turned on the television. His eyes were riveted to cartoons.

Gary arrived. My arms were heavy as sandbags as I tried to hug him. A few minutes later a doctor came in and explained the suspected diagnosis and answered our questions as best he could. I quickly discovered how little was known.

After the doctor left, Gary leaned over to give me a kiss. "Where are Vanessa and Kyeong Sook?' he asked.

"Uh oh," I said. "I'd better go home and check on them." I was glad Gary was paying attention; I'd forgotten all about Vanessa and Kyeong Sook. They were still at the neighbor's house where I'd left them hours ago.

"Mom, bring Small Bear when you come back in the morning." Jay said in a clear voice. Small Bear was the little teddy bear Jay received on his first Christmas in America. The bear had been with him through all five syndactyly release surgeries.

SURGERY WAS SCHEDULED FOR noon on Tuesday. The next three days passed in a blur. On Tuesday morning Jay was prepared for surgery and we waited. I read Jay a story. We played cards. At eleven-thirty our friend Dave, tall and slender, with a careful brown beard and a ready laugh, dropped by. Dave's presence was like a life raft for Gary and me to grab onto. Then, too soon, it was time for surgery. The nurses dressed Small Bear in a makeshift hospital gown, and they wheeled Jay's bed through big double doors, out of sight.

Dave stayed with us, and we sat in the hospital cafeteria. A short while later Gary's mother arrived; her chestnut eyes behind wire rim glasses were kind and apologetic. At three o'clock our friend Ellen arrived with bread, cheese and berries from her garden. She'd guessed correctly that we hadn't bothered to eat lunch.

At a quarter to six the doctor came out of surgery exhausted, yet obviously quite happy.

"The biopsy came back malignant," he said, "but the good news is that I got out all of the tumor. Usually this kind of tumor doesn't remove easily, but this one lifted right out." His face was radiant.

Even though I'd suspected what the outcome of my son's diagnostic test would be, the diagnosis confirming cancer came as a shock.


GARY AND I TOOK TURNS SITTING beside Jay's hospital bed. He had been removed from intensive care, yet he lay small and still underneath the white blankets. He spoke occasionally in soft whispers, but most of the time he slept. Half of his head had been shaved, and his remaining black hair feathered over the white bandage across the back of his head. A needle poked into his hand, and plastic tubes connected him to life. Chemotherapy drugs became familiar to me.

A shunt had been surgically inserted because hydrocephalus from the tumor persisted after surgery. The shunt functioned as a drain inside the body. The tube diverted the excess fluid from Jay's brain and into his abdomen where the fluid was then absorbed by his body. Gary and I found our role with the doctors; we became a team. We were taught how to watch for shunt malfunction and infection.

One afternoon a large group of men and women knocked on the door and entered Jay's hospital room. They explained that they were from a Korean church in a nearby town and had heard we were here. The pastor of the church asked if he could say a prayer for Jay. The prayer was spoken in Korean, and each word first intimated, and then instructed my heart. While I could not understand the exact translation, the love and caring came through powerfully strong. I slid my eyes open and caught a side glanced at Jay. His eyelids were squeezed tightly shut but I could tell he was awake, listening.

After the prayer ended the group departed.

My grandmother telephoned long distance. "I've put Jay on a prayer line," she said. I put down the phone and sat there staring into space, the space beyond the hospital window across summer rain-soaked green grass, to where it blended with mud and eucalyptus trees. Gary dabbed at Jay's forehead with a cold damp washcloth. I spooned a bite of green Jell-O into Jay's mouth; he slurped at it gratefully, but refused a second bite. Moments for Gary and I to be alone together were rare. In the hospital hallway we hugged each other and cried.

Visitors dropped by, each with a gift. Helium balloons danced against the ceiling, and a heaping stack of gift-wrapped packages sat next to Jay's bed unopened.

Kyeong Sook wound a blue curly ribbon around her index finger. "How come nobody is opening up Jay's presents?" Her lips were pressed in a pout. "It's hot outside," she said. "I want to go swimming."

"I could open up Jay's presents for him," Vanessa offered. "Then when he wakes up, he will see them and be happy."

"It's not fair for Vanessa to open up all of the presents. I want to open some too," Kyeong Sook whimpered.

"Let's wait to let Jay open his own presents," Gary said, and he put the stack of packages on a table near the wall.

At a time when many difficult decisions regarding Jay's medical care needed to be made, recurring concerns signaled to me that Kyeong Sook needed help too. She'd begun throwing tantrums again. She was reacting to the fear and stress caused by Jay's illness with anger. She had become demanding, irritable and rebellious.

I could sit back and complain that somebody traumatized her before she came to us. But it didn't seem to make any difference. She was mine now. Mine when she was generous and loving, and mine when she was a little hellion kicking and screaming to have her own way. Yet I knew she was not really a little hellion; she was suffering, just as we all were. Not knowing what else to do, I decided we simply needed more time to bond. And time was the one thing we didn't have.

During the day Kyeong Sook and Vanessa each stayed with a girlfriend. I was lucky that both of my daughters had friends with kind, responsible parents who were willing to care for my children. It was the only arrangement available since both Gary's mother and my mother lived out of town, and they both work full-time.

Gary and I took turns spending the night with Jay at the hospital. On my nights to be at home, I usually picked up my daughters in the evening, we had dinner together, and I made an attempt at ordinary life for a few hours. I read bedtime stories even though by now both girls had outgrown this nightly ritual. For an hour each night we sank into the fantasyland of a book where cancer and brain tumors didn't exist.

When it was Gary's turn to sleep at the hospital, he slept on a cot next to Jay's hospital bed, and after Jay fell asleep, Gary would call me on the telephone. It was as if we'd suddenly awakened and realized that there was nobody waiting to make everything all right for us. We felt like we were the only two people in the world who knew this deep level of pain. After we hung up I cried until my eyes were fiery red, and then I fell asleep.

In the middle of the night Vanessa leaned over my bed. It was three o'clock in the morning.

"I've got a bad pain in my chest," She said.

"Lie down with me for a while," I said.

She pulled the blankets tightly around her and she was shivering.

"It's my heart," Vanessa whispered, "I think it's breaking. I'm scared Jay is going to die." My mind stumbled, came up short, unprepared. I opened my mouth, cleared my throat, "So am I," I replied. I pulled her close and rubbed her back for a long time.

I had fallen into a deep sleep, with Vanessa still at my side when the telephone rang and jolted me awake. Sunlight filled the room;

I answered the phone, heavy with sleep, thinking it was Gary calling from the hospital.

Instantly I recognized the deep voice. It was my friend Chris calling from New Mexico.

"I just want you to know we will be praying for Jay in the Sweat Lodge today," he said. I put down the phone after that nearly wordless conversation. I'd known Chris since I was sixteen.

The Korean community was praying for Jay, there was the prayer line linking across the United States, and now I knew Jay would be prayed for in the ancient way in the sweat lodge ceremony. Sunlight stretched across the wood floor, and the bedroom felt warm and cozy.

An hour later I dropped my daughters off at their friend's house, drove to the hospital and began my day with Jay. When Jay napped, the pale yellow walls of the hospital room seemed to grow smaller, making the room feel even more claustrophobic. I walked down five flights of stairs and paged through the heavy blue-bound books in the basement medical library in order to understand the information provided by the doctors.

An anaplastic ependymoma tumor, I learned, can appear in the brain or spinal cord. Jay's tumor was located in the posterior fossa; the place where it most frequently occurred in younger children. The symptoms of these tumors were flu-like; nausea, vomiting, headaches, and ataxia (unsteady gait). A few weeks earlier Jay had been sick with what we thought was the flu, and for a couple of weeks following he'd had headaches. I'd taken him to have his eyes examined because I thought he might need glasses.

The medical books said that ependymomas were graded by cell type, and low-grade tumors were the easiest to cure. Jay's tumor was a high grade; he had received a high score on the most important test of his life. Surgery alone was rarely curative; patients with these rare, malignant tumors needed to receive whole brain radiation and radiation to the spine due to the tendency for the tumor to spread. It was a recurring kind of tumor, and chemotherapy followed radiation. I read the paragraph on survival rates, and the truth cut into me.

WHEN JAY WAS RELEASED FROM the hospital I knew I had to pull myself together, and by the time we got home, I was actually feeling pretty lucky we'd made it through such a terrible ordeal. I knew we still had a long road ahead filled with radiation, chemotherapy, fear and pain, yet it had begun to dawn on me to look for good things to balance out the bad.

We stepped out of the car and sea air blew in our faces, a tangle of blue morning glories had grown wildly on the front gate and welcomed us. Friends and neighbors dropped by bringing us chicken casseroles, and our church friends brought us bowls of home-cooked Korean foods. Jay was skinny and frail, almost unrecognizable due to the chemotherapy drugs.

July arrived in full force with a heat wave.

"All of my friends have a bikini," Kyeong Sook informed me. She was almost fourteen, and she continued to bite down hard on the notion that I didn't want her. We were still working with a family therapist. I knew her intense emotions overwhelmed her. That since she didn't believe she was loved and wanted, without that safe presence, she could not allow herself to feel. She expressed herself by alternating between angry outbursts, or she clammed up for days at a time. Even though she was deeply concerned about Jay, her thinking tended to be highly self-centered; she found it hard to see beyond her own loss and pain.

Family therapy had taught me that I could not change who she was or the way she dealt with the pain in her life. The best I could do was to be available when she decided to talk with me. I slipped away from the house for an hour to take her shopping. She bought a lime-green bikini.

The next day she pranced out the door, off to the beach. When her friends met her at the edge of the lawn, I caught a glimpse of the frown on her girlfriends' faces. Kyeong Sook was unaware that her shapely legs and lean brown stomach had turned her girlfriends green with envy. But the boys were smiling.

I settled for an hour of beach time late in the afternoon, when the sun was low, and it was safe for Jay to be outside. I was determined to keep our lives as ordinary as possible.


TEN-YEAR-OLD VANESSA PICKED strawberries, and Gary whipped up a pint of cream. We rented videos, checked stacks of books out of the library, and I read to Jay. I wanted to keep our minds from hurling themselves into the fears of the unknown. I found myself wishing for things that never seemed to happen. I wished one of Jay's friends would invite him over for a play date and that he would have enough energy to play, or that someone would invite our family over for a barbecue.

Weeks folded into months. Jay had thirty days of whole brain radiation, followed by many cycles of chemotherapy. He looked like a wisp of life. He had a puffy face and stood on thin bird legs. Mostly he languished on the couch, seldom playing at all.

Often I put Jay in a wheelchair and we went for long walks.

"Ice cream would sure taste good." Jay looked at me waiting for my response.

"Let's splurge," I said. "Do you want one scoop or two?"

I pushed the wheelchair and Jay sucked at the cone. Chocolate dripped past the white paper napkin, all the way down to his elbows. And while I was slurping away at my scoop of coffee ice cream, and marveling at how good I was getting at staying in the moment, enjoying a delightful slice of the day, Jay leaned over and threw up. I wiped his mouth with a damp napkin.

His once beautiful black hair was beginning to fall out due to radiation. Each time I brushed my hand across his head dry tufts of hair landed on his shoulders. We pretended not to notice the stares we got when we were out in public. Periodic vomiting continued. The medicine that was supposed to make the cancer go away was the same medicine that made Jay helplessly sick. Because Jay had an aggressive, recurring type of tumor the doctors suspected the tumor might grow back at any time. He was monitored closely. I just hung on to the belief that the healthy cells would regenerate and hoped that the cancer cells wouldn't.

"You look great and you're so strong," my friends said. It made me feel super human at a time when I wanted to feel ordinary.

"Look beyond my freshly washed hair, behind my mascara rimmed eyes to where my mind aches," I told them.

"Of course, I can't possibly imagine what it's like for you," another friend told me.

"Yes you can," I insisted. "Close your eyes and pretend it's your child; that deep dark hole you're afraid of falling into is the same one I'm looking down."

Our family began attending monthly childhood cancer support group meetings. While Gary and I sat in a circle and talked with other parents, Vanessa, Kyeong Sook and Jay participated in a kids support group activity. It gave us a chance to get to know other families with lives similar to ours.

## ﹦ FALL, 1991 ﹦

By now Gary was back into his regular work routine, I didn't even try. I telephoned the Visiting Nurses and made arrangements to keep the wheelchair. Snarled fishing line and sandy beach towels cluttered the front porch. A man came to fix the washing machine, and women called from the Make-A-Wish Foundation, an organization that grants wishes to kids with a life threatening illness.

"Yep, you can wish for anything you want," we told Jay. His chin quivered. He was bone thin.

"Wish for a trip to Disney World," Kyeong Sook told him.

Jay struggled to sit up.

"Jay, you're a lucky boy. You get to wish for anything you want." Gary brushed his hand across the top of Jay's head; wisps of baby-fine black hair had begun growing in.

A television show we watched a year or two ago flashed through my mind. It was an episode about children dying from cancer and receiving a final wish. I wasn't sure if Jay remembered seeing the program, yet I decided not to take the chance.

"It doesn't mean you are going to die." I said. "They've changed those wish programs. Nowadays any kid with cancer gets to make a wish, even the ones that get better."

It took Jay a couple of weeks to decide on the perfect wish. He chose to go to a toy store and buy anything he wanted. Yet by now Jay's energy level was so low all he wanted to do was sleep. He did his best to shop and select toys, but he became exhausted after half an hour. In the end he was content to bring home a small selection of computer games and some Legos. The Make-A-Wish staff said that Jay was the least greedy child they'd ever met. In truth he was probably one of the sickest children they had ever met, because when he was feeling well Jay could out-shop anybody.

Most days Jay threw up much of what he ate. He refused the stories I wanted to read to him, and he had lost interest in watching television. His healthy cells had been knocked around, and his lowered blood counts brought about an anemia, which made him constantly cold even though the weather was warm outside. When I brought this to the attention of our team of doctors they shrugged it off as a normal side effect of chemotherapy and radiation.

Jay had lost all hope; he had just given up. I wanted to give up too, but I never quite figured out how to do it. At my lowest point, I sat outside on the grass and asked God to help Jay or to "take him." When I say God I don't mean a single Christian concept of God. I mean Creator, The Great Spirit, Grandfather Spirit; the presence that guides us in a sacred manner.

Later that same day Jay got up out of bed, and he got dressed. The shine was back in his eyes. He was still weak, but he wanted to know if we could go to the library and check out books.

The following week Jay and I began going down to the creek behind our house. There was only a trickle of water with a broad sandy bank. We put a mound of birdseed on the ground and hid in the bushes and watched scrub jays pick out sunflower seeds.

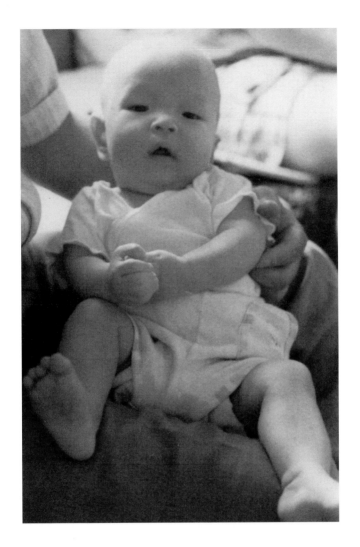

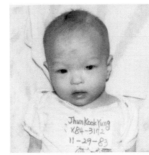

*Jay in Korea, 1984.*

*Jay and Vanessa, 1985.*

*Vanessa, Terra, Gary and Jay, 1986.*

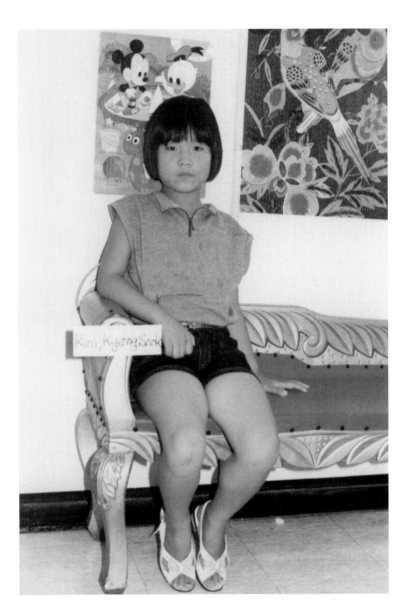

*Kyeong Sook in Korea, 1987.*

*Kyeong Sook's first day with us, 1987.*

*Kyeong Sook and Vanessa. First afternoon together.*

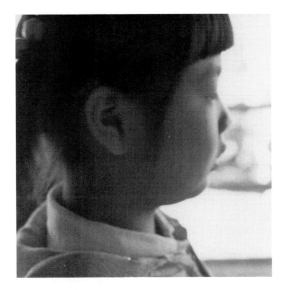

*Kyeong Sook, 1988.*

*Gary and me, 1988.*

*Kyeong Sook, Jay and Vanessa, rolling in the sand at the beach.*

*Vanessa and Kyeong Sook with friends, 1989.*

*Kyeong Sook, Vanessa, Gary, Jay and our dog Sadie.*

*Jay, Ahryun and me, 1990.*

*Vanessa and Tanna, 1990.*

*Gary with Korean
community
members, 1991.*

*Kyeong Sook, Jay and Vanessa, 1991.*

*Trevor family with Korean community church members, 1991.*

*Terra with dyed blond hair, and Jay without hair, 1991.*

*Jay and Gary. Jay's last cycle of chemotherapy.*

*Jay, rebounding after the long cancer journey, with our dog Sadie, 1993.*

*Jay, Kyeong Sook, Vanessa, and our dog Sadie.*

*Vanessa
and Sadie.*

*Trevor family, 1995.*

*Vanessa, Jay and me, at Mt. St. Helen's, 1997.*

*Trevor family, 1997.*

*Jay, 1998.*

*Gary and Vanessa, 2003.*

*Kyeong Sook and me, 2003.*

Another day we heard a rustle in the deep grass. Something black poked out a shiny black nose. It was a mamma skunk, with five babies in tow. They filed past us, ever so watchful; ready to respond to the slightest movement. We sat silent, barely daring to breathe, watching them drink from the creek.

That fall the weather was wonderful. There were days that just demanded you be outside; it was neither warm nor cold, the air was perfect. The creek bed was still my strongest medicine and the place Jay and I went for spur-of-the-moment visits with nature.

"Do you want to make a wish, Mom?" Jay asked. He leaned down and plucked dried dandelion blossoms. When he stood up the knees of his gray sweatpants were streaked with brown dirt. He kicked at a pile of leaves; the laces on his red tennis shoes were untied. Then he wobble-skipped over to where I was standing.

"What did you wish for?" I asked after he had blown the fluff off of the dandelion he was holding. "To go to Korea," he said. "Mom, do you think that someday you could take me to Korea?"

"I hope so." I bent down next to Jay, and kissed his cheek.

Jay's brain tumor chemotherapy continued for eighteen long months. Sometimes his blood count got so low procedures had to be delayed for much longer than was expected. Finally he reached the end of treatment. We took a picture of Jay receiving his last cycle of chemo. The medical clinic gave him a farewell gift. We went home and packed up all the medical supplies, and let Jay flush all of his leftover medications down the toilet. I felt like the sun had come out after a blizzard. Then we celebrated the end of a long journey. Yet finishing treatment was also very difficult. Chemo was over, but cancer was still a part of our lives. I knew we would always live with the fear of relapse.

We held our breath. What if the brain tumor came back, dragging us away again? Each day, when it didn't happen, I gained more confidence.

Slowly Jay began to gain more energy and feel stronger. I felt a sense of liberation, a sense of getting on with the rest of our lives.

## ⋛ WINTER OF HOPE, 1993 ⋚

Jay was bouncing back, and my cousin Victor was going through a stretch of time when AIDS made him feel less sick. He wasn't healthy like I usually feel; his good health was more like when I had a bad case of the flu. A few days after Christmas I flew to midstate Oregon to visit him. Besides being cousins we were soul mates. That weekend I slept on a window seat bed with white linen sheets, a white down comforter lightly scented in bleach. My view overlooked a forest of pine trees covered with snow. Usually Victor slept in this bed, and while I was there he struggled upstairs to sleep in the loft.

All weekend we cooked our meals together. Cooking together meant Victor washed the shrimp, de-veined them, chopped the swiss chard, got the water boiling for pasta, then he ran out of energy and from a rocking chair told me how to assemble the rest of the meal.

Victor had full-blown AIDS. Already he had lived many years longer than doctors had predicted. Of course I knew my cousin was going to die. He was comfortable talking about dying, but he was also busy living.

At four o'clock in the morning, when both of us couldn't sleep, Victor served me coffee in bed. We lit dozens of white candles and talked until the sun came up and we let ourselves feel something that felt like ghost spirits leave the room. Still I was like a little girl, not really believing his death would happen.

All weekend we lived a fairy tale. A group of dear friends rented a dog sled complete with a guide to take us mushing. Victor, wearing two sets of long underwear under his clothes, rode in the canvas-covered basket, while I balanced my feet on the narrow sled in the front with the driver.

Saturday morning we had to spend an hour at the hospital while Victor went through a decontamination procedure, but this was ordinary stuff for my cousin.

He joked, "I've given up flossing my teeth to make room in my schedule for more doctor's appointments."

Not flossing teeth because they would not be needed for much longer was almost impossible for me to grasp. I was forty years old at the time, and so far no one I'd loved had ever died. The threat of death was everywhere in my life, yet it hadn't happened. After the decontamination appointment, Victor grabbed my arm. "I'm supposed to meet with a mortician this afternoon. I'd like you to come with me. "

I tensed and tightened my toes. "Yeah, I want to go with you." I said.

"Are you sure? It'll be pretty emotional."

"Yeah, I said again. I want to go." The snow tires clicked over the road. I glanced out the window; we were surrounded by snow-covered pine trees shimmering in the sunlight. The roads were icy. By the time we arrived at the mortuary, faint lines of silver shone through a darkening sky.

We stamped snow from our boots, and my cousin opened the door. The room smelled of lilacs. I timidly peered around the corner;

the mortician, dressed in jeans and a blue flannel shirt came out to greet us.

"Sorry about my appearance." He offered. "I don't usually dress so casual."

"I'm glad you're not wearing a suit," I told him. I was developing laryngitis and my throat ached.

"We spoke on the phone yesterday," Victor said, and then he added, "I'm looking for a pine coffin." I stared at my cousin, my age, struggling to stand up. I thought about the day before, sitting with Victor on the couch, my feet in his lap, both of us laughing.

We were led down a narrow hall to a large room filled with coffins. There were metal coffins made of copper, bronze, a choice of leather or velvet interior.

"This looks like an automobile showroom on the moon," I blurted out. "I would be caught—"

"Dead in one of these." Victor finished my sentence for me and laughed. "That's why it's important to choose your own." His laughter helped me relax.

A pine coffin sat near the back of the room, almost out of sight. Slowly, gently, I ran my fingers across the wood, a choke swelled in my throat. Tears began to sting and I willed them to stay in my eyes. My cousin pulled me close, and put his arm around me, our eyes met. I took a deep breath, and let the tears roll off my chin.

The next day Victor lost his balance coming down the stairs. He fell on top of his eleven-foot-tall, carefully decorated Christmas tree. Our eyes met, I helped him up. This time we couldn't laugh or even cry.

All weekend we shared the same tiny bathroom; we used separate towels for drying our hands. While lying awake for most of a night in my cousin's bed with white moonlight in my face, I got scared and panicky. It was 1993, and although by then it was medically proven *impossible*, buried in my heart was the secret fear of somehow bringing the HIV virus home with me. Jay's health was still so fragile. What if I somehow managed to give AIDS germs to Jay?

That night I got up at least fifteen times to go to the bathroom, nerves ripped through my stomach. The small sound of an owl pushed against the night. I wanted to be fearless, but even with all of my great medically backed knowledge; I had to settle for being brave.

## SPRING, 1993

In the past I often worked extra hard to keep our house clean. Suddenly, gone forever were my mindless ways of griping about toys scattered all over the living room. Now I treasured those heaps of clutter left lying about. The saddest time of my life had been when Jay was too sick to play. His toys sat orderly, unplayed with, and his spic-and-span bedroom had a lonely, vacant feel to it.

Now Jay's wooden train track wound around the couch, crossed under my desk and it didn't bother me at all. Not even at night when I got out of bed and knocked my toe into the train watchman shack. Carefully I vacuumed around all the little curved and straight pieces of track.

I shut off the vacuum cleaner. Why bother? The day after tomorrow all the grime and grit would return, and after the dog gave one big shake, hairballs would collect under the chairs again. It seemed unthinkable to leave our dog Sadie outside when she wanted to be inside the house with us. Dog hair on the floor was no longer a big deal, and then I made a mental note of all the things that didn't bother me any more.

I opened the back door. Eucalyptus was thick in the air, and from high up in a tree branch a red-tailed hawk gazed down at me.

Around my feet orange poppies reached toward the sun. I sprawled on the grass, the sun felt wonderful on my back, and I just lay there grinning.

"What are you doing?" Vanessa asked.

"Nothing," I said. "I've got spring fever."

"Mom, that's just a joke. It's not something people can catch."

Vanessa sat on the grass. She had just returned from the beach and she was wearing a pink bathing suit. Her body reminded me of a young gazelle. She brushed a strand of hair from her face. Her hair had darkened to brown and matched her eyes, but the ends were still honey blond. She was almost twelve, and already she was as tall as I was. She seemed so much older than I was at her age. Then I remembered how much living had been crammed into her life. She was three and a half when Jay joined our family. She adored her new baby brother fresh off the plane from Korea.

I'd tested her faith again at age six when I gave her an older sister. Now Vanessa was learning about cancer and brain tumors.

The hawk turned his head from left to right, blinking. Vanessa yawned.

"Sadie, come here girl." Vanessa called. The dog groaned as she moved herself onto all fours, then lumbered over to her. She dropped to the ground at Vanessa's feet and rolled over, belly up.

"Do you want a scratch?" Vanessa cooed.

"Isn't that a new bathing suit?" I asked.

Vanessa stood up and twirled around, "It's a hand-me down, Rylee's mother gave it to me. My old one was so small it couldn't stretch to fit me anymore."

## ≿ WINTER, 1994 ≾

Frequently we received letters from our friends Ahryun and Tanna who now lived in Sweden. We had formed a close friendship in the summer of 1990 when they stayed with us. Vanessa and Tanna exchanged letters and photos on a regular basis. Ahryun and I wrote to each other regularly as well.

"It's snowing and dark, even in the daytime," Ahryun wrote. "Tanna has begun school, and it is very near our home. It takes two or three minutes on foot. She and her sister have learned to ice skate, and each day they skate together."

Ahryun always ended each letter by saying, "Make a trip to Sweden."

I began to feel concerned after a long stretch of time went by without any word; usually they wrote quite regularly. Then came the phone call saying Tanna was dead.

Gary answered the phone. It was a Saturday morning, and I was out running errands. All morning, at the post office, the grocery store, while I filled the gas tank in my car, I had felt uneasy. It was a warning sensation, a foreboding feeling, and I knew that something had happened, but I had no idea what.

When I got home Gary met me at the front door and gave me the news. My fingers were shaking as I dialed Ahryun's phone number. What do you say to a mother whose child has just died? I was afraid of saying the wrong thing, but mostly I was afraid of being around so much pain and sorrow.

When Ahryun answered the phone the gift of articulate speech still had not come to me. I struggled along feeling my way with each word.

Ahryun spoke first. "I'm so sorry I've been avoiding you. I stopped writing to you because I was so afraid to find out if Jay died. And now it's Tanna." Her voice broke off. We both cried forever so long, then for an immeasurable amount of time we were both profoundly silent. The silence stretched all the way from Stockholm to California. This silence came with a set of reassuring answers. It gave strength, that vital life force which enables us to hold each other up. It was the perfect equilibrium that no words could ever match.

Ahryun told me the span of Tanna's last few months and about the day she died on an icy highway, in a car crash. She said Tanna had been talking about Vanessa early that very morning, and that she had been so happy, and in a bubbly cheerful mood, on the last day of her life.

I tensed my shoulders, listening with the ear of a mother who was afraid her own child might have to make that same journey to heaven.


VANESSA COULD NOT ACCEPT Tanna's death. This kind of thing didn't happen very often to children, as far as she knew. But if it could happen to Tanna, it could happen to Jay, or to anyone. The happier she tried to be, the harder she tried to play, the further away the pain seemed to stay. She kept up an almost frantic pace, and then finally she began her grieving process by writing a letter to Tanna to say goodby.

Soon after Vanessa developed an interest in pow wow dancing. She didn't participate in the competitions. She danced the more casual intertribal where all of the dancers came together. I watched Vanessa fold her blue shawl over her arm. I knew she was a little bit nervous, yet we did not talk. Silence was our conversation, and it told me more than words. We sat a few paces behind the hay bales and were careful to keep our feet and legs a safe distance away from bustles, eagle feathers and other people's regalia.

First there was a ground blessing, then the flag bearers led with the American flag, the state flag and an Eagle Staff. Next began the Grand Entry with the dancers representing many different tribes. I watched Vanessa enter the dance arena with a group of children. After all the dancers were in the arbor a flag song was sung, then a prayer was offered, followed by a victory song.

An intertribal song began with hundreds of soft moccasins dancing. Young men, teenage boys, girls fancy dancing, the elders who barely moved and kept their feet close to the earth.

In the dance arena under a sky blue as turquoise, I pulled my shawl up around my shoulders, I felt the drum, and then it was just like what Amy Tan said about visiting China. For me, the moment my feet touched the earth in dance I felt Indian.

In the dance arena no one rushed. Each step was done with care. After that long pow wow weekend Vanessa moved through her days unhurried. As that pow wow season and the next one passed, her frantic pace halted.

# ⇒ SPRING, 1995 ⇐

Blue lupine grew thick near the edge of the driveway in good rich spring light; the winter slant was gone. The air was just right for remembering June was on its way. Jay was almost eleven, and he was four years past diagnosis. He had gained thirty pounds; the episodes of vomiting were gone. Course black hair grew everywhere on his head except on the back of his head where the tumor had been removed.

Jay was healthy again. When he came home from school his face was sweaty, the knees of his jeans were streaked with grass stains. Gone were the pristine sick days when his white hooded sweatshirt stayed spotlessly clean for weeks at a time. I'd climbed out of the space where all of his medical problems were filed in my mind. Each time he left a muddy footprint on the kitchen floor I rejoiced; it felt so good to have a healthy kid again.

Gary and Jay developed a love for fishing, and they began to spend lots of long Saturdays out on the ocean. One weekend on a fishing trip, Gary caught so many yellowtail his shoulder stiffened from hauling those big yellows in. Good fishing weather had become so important to Gary that he studied the clouds, scrutinized the sunsets as well as the dawns. Jay gauged the winds and collected tackle boxes, rods and reels. Gary began collecting great fish recipes and began to do lots of cooking. His perfect cioppino soup always received rave reviews. Though Jay was his constant fishing companion it wasn't long before Gary began making friends with some of the men in the Asian deep-sea fishing community. Once in a while Kyeong Sook fished too. Having spent her early childhood living on the coast of Yosu in South Korea where everyone in her growing-up family made their living from the sea, fishing came naturally to her, and it soothed her.

As summer deepened on the days when Jay wasn't fishing, we began getting up earlier than usual to check on the creek behind our house. My knee-high rubber boots pushed deep into the rain-soaked soil. We spotted milky white stones, round and endless. Usually our walks by the creek were squeezed into the week whenever we could manage.

Lately we'd become a little bit too ordinary. In the cancer days we never put fun on the back burner. In the beginning, when Jay first began to recover from cancer, I went around feeling glad all the time. I appreciated him so much, I couldn't take my eyes off him. It was a huge thing to have my child alive. The cancer part was dreadful, but I felt such a desperate love it was always a glitter moment. After a while so much gladness became awful. Then the good part started; I began to feel ordinary, and we could postpone things. We were regular people again.

What's new, however, was that my son was a survivor of an anaplastic ependymoma, grade IV, brain tumor, leaving me less sure of the answers than I had ever been before. There is not a better prize than being an average mother and son out for a morning walk. For a portion of each creek visit I stayed at least forty paces away from where Jay explored. I watched his face discover tail-drag marks and footprints. At last my curiosity to learn what he could see, overcame my desire to let my son explore these city-woods all by himself. I crossed the creek, stepping firmly into the ankle deep water.

Jay's feet had finally begun to grow like boys' feet ought to. They had grown so much he was wearing my rubber boots, leaving me to force my feet into a smaller pair well worn by Jay and both of his older sisters. I enjoyed the feel of the stream against my booted legs.

"Be careful, mom." Jay shouted from the other side of the bank. His voice was low, slightly embarrassed-sounding. At once I felt the gush of icy water melt into my sock.

A palpable energy hovered in Jay's voice. "I forgot to tell you, there is a hole in the left boot," he said.

I paused theatrically, and then sat down at the edge of the stream bank and dumped water out of my boot. Then I let him see my grinning face. Usually I spent plenty of time pouring water out of a boot I'd mistakenly thought taller than the water was deep.

Sometimes our dog Sadie came with us. Being a typical New-foundland, on cool mornings she felt expansive, and puppy-like. We'd throw a stick for her to fetch, and she'd put her head all the way under the water until it was located. The game lasted only a few minutes, and then she went to get the stick and put it down with a glance that said not to go bothering her to retrieve it again, because she was busy now lying on her belly in a patch of shade.

Jay and I sat and listened to the buzzing of grasshopper wings, and there were stories I told him about growing up in the mountains, when I roamed fearless in the 1960s, when creek beds and vacant lots still belonged to nature and children. Our creek time gave us a chance to be together in a relaxed way.

This youngest child of mine was in no hurry to grow up. To him mothers were still wonderful companions. He had a basic trust to the nth degree. His heart was a river of pure light; childhood curiosity seldom took him into the twilight zone of bad judgment. So when this great idea came to me, I couldn't stop myself. I splashed, jumped, kicked at the water with all my passion, and then sat down in the middle of the creek. Jay stared at me with wide brown eyes brimming with question marks, his face pinched with confusion.

"Can I do it too, or do you think it might make me get sick?"

"Go for it," I coaxed. "You're healthy now. It won't hurt you."

At once he flopped down next to me in the icy water, leaning his back into the gentle flow, grinning, his eyes shinning like two polished stones. Next he filled his long black rubber boot with water and dangled it over my head.

"Do you dare me to pour this on you, Mom?" Even when teasing, this child felt the world with his heart.

The creek that flowed through our backyard was a playground without equal. It had everything a child needed; elderly oak, columns of eucalyptus teeming with red-tail hawks, and owls. But it was also a hazard. There were telltale signs—mud-encrusted trash and beer cans. We made a small pile of what ought not to be there and carried it home to our garbage can.

Each day we checked the water level. After each rainstorm the creek looked very different. Carefully, Jay recorded his discoveries in a spiral-bound notebook: Clear water before the first rain. The second day it was muddy, then clear on the third day, but now there was a layer of smooth burgundy mud. With a metal spatula (the kind used to turn pancakes) Jay lifted a raccoon fingerprint out of the mud and placed it on a white paper plate.

We went to the creek day after day. Then one morning the creek was back to only a trickle of water, and the streambed had become a broad sandy bank. Where the ground once absorbed water, it now gave a home to healthy golden dandelions, springing thick and sudden. As I stood in awe, feeling small, concentrating on this mysterious gift, I let myself know what was at the edge of my mind; Jay was starting puberty. I knew because breast buds were forming. Some boys grow breasts in adolescence.

I climbed back into the space in my mind where my son's medical problems were filed away. Why must he also have the burden of a full chest? There was a dark shadow across his upper lip, and blackheads on his nose.

No. My mind screamed. Let him keep his childhood for a while longer.

The radiologist's words, almost forgotten, return, and now I understand what he meant for me to hear. Again the nuclear statement was fired at me, and it is as if I am hearing, rather than remembering the doctor's words. "Whole brain radiation in children under seven causes marked learning disabilities."

At the time I brushed the statement off. The words came at me like mosquitoes buzzing and biting. My only hope then was for Jay to live. Greedily I prayed to be lucky enough to one day cope with the problems our doctor outlined.

At age seven and a half Jay had received fifty-four gray (5400 rad) to the posterior fossa. Thirty-six gray (3600 rad) to the croniospinal axis, all between July 16 and August 28, 1991. The day the team of experts charted Jay's course, I sat on a tall bar stool in the radiology lab, listening in a way that recorded information I would only be capable of understanding four years later. I sat snacking on the M & Ms that were being passed around, pretending I wasn't sick out of my mind with worry.

My act worked. I looked like an extra technician or a student observing and was allowed to stay in the room with Jay while the radiologist and a crew of others began to chart his treatment course. Medical terms were casually flung around the room, along with statements like, "Too bad his tumor is a high grade and we have to give him such a huge dose of radiation." All the while I kept my mind clamped shut. I was in never-never land, a place that didn't allow my son to have any of those late effects of whole brain radiation. Always I was mistaken for somebody else.

"You are his mother? I had no idea; you seem so calm." And that's how it all began; I was the calm lady with a great haircut and stylish clothes on the outside. On the inside I'd lost my normal capacity for listening. The real me should have been reported as a missing person.

Because I've recently come into possession of a red tail hawk nest which blew out of a tree, and landed at my feet. I've come to think of those early days as my own nest. It was a safe space of time where I could mend, and grow strong again. The bird's nest I have is obviously old. The baby birds had flown away; the nest was no longer needed. Now that I no longer needed the safety of denial, I was able to remember everything I'd been told about Jay's long-term disabilities.

Usually I went around being so glad my son was surviving an aggressive form of cancer. But lately, a few times each day, the information of how very lucky we were lifted and I remembered that Jay's brain had been rearranged from a brain tumor, and radiation. He probably wouldn't be able to drive a train when he grew up like he was hoping, but maybe he could be the conductor.

My mind raced back to the quiet space remembering the difficulty Jay was having in school. It was hard to keep on pretending his mind would go back to the way it was. After chemotherapy ended he had repeated the first grade and for a while he seemed to be doing OK. But now, even with the help of a special resource teacher, Jay wasn't always able to keep up with the rest of the class. He understood what he was supposed to do, yet his thought process was much slower than average. He wrote slowly and needed extra time to complete assignments.

For children under seven, whole brain radiation makes learning to read and write a burdensome task. Fortunately Jay's penmanship was perfect and he was already an exceptionally good reader at age seven and a half "before" receiving his lifetime dose of radiation. I didn't want to remember that children under seven who received cranial radiation were often the victims of IQ loss. An average full-scale IQ of 115 at diagnosis could fall to 90 by the second year. It didn't help to remember that Jay had started out with a high IQ. My heart trembled at the unfairness of it all.

When they are trying to rid your child of cancer nobody actually comes right out and says, "Hey this might make him well, but it's also going to give him lots of other problems, too." No one explains how much it will change your child's life. Naturally it won't change things nearly as much as death, which is what would probably happen if you didn't do the whole brain radiation and chemotherapy.

At your very first appointment they don't pass out maps or give you any guidebooks. They just begin telling you things that are bound to happen, but they tell you all this right after you've been told that your child has cancer and at that point you aren't doing your best job of listening. The only part, which truly registers, is that your child's hair will fall out. Then you feel really silly because the only important thing is keeping your child alive.

It might occur to the doctors to say, "Hey, come back when all of this applies to you, and we will explain all those long-term problems to you again." Instead they just look at you with those mind-numbing sad eyes, and you're supposed to *know*.

It didn't matter. Radiation had saved Jay' life and we had puberty ahead. Each time one of my children had began puberty; I felt caught in my own helplessness. Kyeong Sook and Vanessa had leaped into this passage; I ought to know what it's all about. I did know, in my bones I remembered, yet knowing as their mother was more complex. Kyeong Sook hit puberty like a runaway train only nine months after becoming my daughter. I missed out on the diaper stage, but arrived in time to buy mini-pads. At best it was confusing. I had short notice, but I knew the rules of conduct. There were plenty of loose conversations; those gentle check-in sessions. Still something went wrong, we never gained a connection to each other.

While puberty isn't raved about at our dinner table, more than other accomplishments, a child's body growing into adulthood is perhaps the most complicated thing that will ever happen to them. With Vanessa, things were a bit less strained. We had time to prepare, but more importantly she was willing to let me be her mother. Still she had her older sister's warnings to match against my carefully chosen words. Within the snatches of conversation I mentioned a tribal tradition of young girls burying their first menstrual period, a ritual practiced by her not-so-distant Cherokee, Delaware and Seneca female ancestors. She went to the tree-lined creek behind our house, and something inside her quieted down.

I accepted it as natural, rather taking for granted the normalcy of puberty changes taking place with my children, but as their mother I was also caught by surprise. My babies were becoming young women. A voice in my head kept pestering me, "Your daughters have fully developed reproductive systems, and how do you feel about it?"

I felt a bit old, not from their passage, but mostly from staring too hard into the mirror. Yet I didn't try to hide my gray hair, I liked it, sort of. With my daughters I shared hormone tears, and laughter. Soon though we would have menstruation backed against menopause.

Even with all this experience, Jay's puberty hit me hard. The thing is, puberty is the loss of contented children whose happiness is best measured by the amount of cookie crumbs packed into the living room sofa. Our family pattern (which has less to do with hereditary factors, and more to do with having children born in autumn months and starting school a bit older) was to become pubescent in the fifth grade. Jay began right on schedule. First the crackly voice, then a dark shadow across his upper lip. He was willing to drop the defenses that had enabled him to survive the hard times in his life, and by the age of eleven he had what I've long searched for, confidence. He walked into the kitchen smiling a Cheshire-cat smile, and said, "Mom, remember all those things you said would happen to me when I was about eleven or twelve? Well, it's starting." His voice was low, but without embarrassment. I nodded, our glances met.

THAT NIGHT VANESSA GAVE HER first boy-girl party. I suppose, to be accurate she invited twenty budding, hormonally challenged adolescents over for pizza. Fourteen-year-olds are like four-year-olds, very sophisticated four-year-olds. At first the boys rolled around on the floor with the dog. The girls made conversation, and every few minutes they giggled and glanced over at the boys. As the seconds pass (time is measured in seconds, not minutes) a question loomed, a palpable presence.

"What should we do?" The kids asked each other. As the embarrassment grew plainer and plainer, their courage grew to meet it. Someone found my clothespins. Hot pink and yellow plastic clothespins. They boys then sportively clipped them onto their ear lobes, congratulating each other, as if they were a treasure everyone had been looking for.

The first awkward moments ended and the gathering took shape. They shaped each other with their actions, with the wear and tear of subtle pressures and laughter. But the real action began when the music was cranked up full volume. It ended the standing around and staring, led directly to girls dancing. The first boy to dance became an instant hero. Other boys joined in rapid succession. A tangle of waving arms and bent-elbows made hieroglyphics in the air.

Adolescence is a time of redoing, but Vanessa's joyous cries of not so long ago, "Watch me, Mommy! Watch me!" turned to looks of disdain whenever I tried to so much as sneak a peek into the living room. The look on her face says it all: "Get lost, Mom." So I promised, as I did every time there are teenage guests, to chaperone from a careful distance.

The rules we set for this get-together were practically the same ones we used for her preschool play dates: monitor the children closely. Either Gary or I walked though the house to get a tube of Chapstick from the bathroom, to open a window, or close the front door.

"Yikes!" Jay said after emerging from the living room with his sister's friends.

"It's nuts in there, they're playing musical chairs." Jay was old enough to want to be rid of me too, but young enough not to realize it yet. For a few minutes he hung out in the kitchen with Gary until the door between the dining room and the kitchen flew open, its loose hinge complaining as Vanessa, shoulders hunched, strode purposefully through. She made a frightening face at her brother,

"We're cutting the cake, so are you coming?"

Admittedly in the beginning I viewed the idea of twenty fourteen-year-olds with mixed emotions. But eighth grade, for me, was about waiting for another perfect cell to form; waiting to be taller, to be prettier. It was about waiting to be picked for teams, and waiting to be asked to parties and about cliques: something wonderful to be in and terrible to be out of. So how in the world could I insist on her having a smaller-end-of-the year graduation party, to ask her to exclude friends she truly liked?

I am wise, but not patient. Three hours passed slower than I would have thought possible. Finally it was ten-thirty, and the parents came to collect their kids. Gary and I paused sleepily at our doorway, soaking up the last few moments of togetherness with all those kids.

"I know!" Vanessa exclaimed breathlessly. "We could do this again on my birthday." I could almost hear the gears in her head turning.

Our old house seemed to sigh along with me as it disgorged the teenagers through the front door.

THE FOLLOWING SATURDAY MORNING Kyeong Sook was home, I had a few unclaimed hours, and I decided to ask her if she wanted to go shopping with me. Kyeong Sook was a junior in high school. Usually she left the house on weekdays at seven-thirty in the morning to attend school. She worked a part-time job after school and on weekends, so we seldom spent time together. Over the years our relationship had not improved, yet it hadn't worsened either. Occasionally she confided to me or asked for my opinion. I had a closer mother-daughter bond with Kyeong Sook than some of my friends had with their daughters, so I knew we fell somewhere in the vicinity of normal. Still it was not as deep a connection as I wanted to have, and I knew she yearned to have a closer tie with me as well. Yet neither of us knew how to bridge the gap, so I was delighted when she agreed to go shopping with me.

The blue dress Kyeong Sook fell in love with reminded me of the kind of silk my great-grandmother used to trim her blankets. She stood at the edge of the dressing room drowsy with possibilities. I buried the thoughts about the sensible everyday clothes we were *supposed* to be buying. The results of sensibility, I reminded myself, were the white Bermuda shorts purchased two summers ago that were never worn.

"You can buy the dress," I said.

Thick black hair fell across Kyeong Sook's shoulders. The morning glory blue material rippled like wind walking across grass.

"But what if something happens, and I do something bad, will I still get to keep the dress?"

"There is nothing you could ever do that would cause me to take this dress away from you. It will be yours no matter what," I said. Unlike her brother who needed to be held lightly, this daughter needed to test the strength of my grip. Kyeong Sook went through long spells where she followed rules and just when it seemed too good to be true the bottom would drop out. The morning she chose to skip school and bring her boyfriend into her bedroom was the same day Gary chose to come home for an early lunch.

Other times she came in late at night long past her curfew. It was as if she needed to do something she wasn't supposed to do in order to prove to herself that she wasn't worthy of being loved. She still worked hard to convince herself that I didn't want her. She no longer screamed at me when she was angry, now she threw silent tantrums; wouldn't talk, wouldn't participate in family activities, sulked at the dinner table and sulked in the bedroom she shared with Vanessa. These episodes lasted for days. Kyeong Sook's negative attitude was crazy-making and kept all of us on edge. Perhaps there is no adequate description for some older-child adoptions, which happen with such a full on force.

When we arrived home from shopping Kyeong Sook put the blue dress on again. She leaned hard into the mirror's reflection, pushing aside all that thick black hair. The mail arrived bringing the latest issue of an adoption newsletter. I glanced at the photos of waiting children—Lisa's high-cheeked face stared at me. She is eight, and has experienced extreme neglect in her birth family. An athletic girl, Lisa enjoys sports, and she also likes to cook and bake, but she can be bossy, and stubborn. It says a two-parent family, where at least one parent is Native American is needed; that she'd do best in a family experienced in parenting children who have been abused and neglected.

Five minutes later I dumped handfuls of birdseed into the feeder. I added an extra helping of sunflower seeds for the scrub jays that send the smaller feed to the ground like rain while searching for their favorite treat. I know the adoption agency was looking for another mom like me, for I know what it is to parent a child whose needs are almost too massive for my strength.

I remember when I used to think that all a troubled child needed was to be brought into a loving family and be loved. Now I know better. I didn't view myself as any different from any other parent, adoptive or not, yet I was bamboozled. Thus far, the bond of trust I needed to establish with Kyeong Sook, wasn't building. What I didn't have with her, I had with Jay, so I knew it had nothing to do with parenting a child who was not genetically related to me. Yet it had everything to do with parenting a teenager who had spent her first ten years, some of the most important years of her life, in multiple foster homes, and an orphanage.

We had years of getting-nowhere counseling. Never one to waste money or admit defeat, I spent those sessions discovering my own thorns; we all have them. An older child adoption required parents to look for resources, and accept help. It demanded multiple, strong support systems. We had to work at creating positive memories, and let go of our expectations. Loss and abandonment issues surfaced when we least expected it.

Holidays and other marker events brought out old sadness from her former family life (things we didn't even know about) and it got mixed up in current family life.

What many people don't know is that masked sadness usually surfaces as anger. Still, there are those of us bound for the older child adoption trail. We saddled up, and got ready to ride. Violet water bathed our thoughts.

# ≳ WINTER, 1995 ≲

Kyeong Sook wrote regularly in a journal, and she kept it in her desk. If I had been a snooping sort of mother, I would have known what was coming next.

December 25, 1995 was a perfect Christmas. It was a cheerful day filled with more joy and relaxed togetherness than usual. Our family shared a laughter filled afternoon and a fun dinner together. Everyone had a great time. So when Kyeong Sook asked to spend the evening with her boyfriend's family, I agreed. Colored lights lined the outside eaves of our house. Inside our Christmas tree glowed with twinkling white lights. There was a fire in the fireplace, and flames leaped up and snapped at the kindling. Vanessa and Jay were flanked across the floor playing a board game. Before bed we watched a television program about angels, missing people and miracles.

Since I didn't expect Kyeong Sook to be home until quite late, at ten thirty p.m. when I was too tired to stay awake any longer, I turned off the Christmas lights, turned on the front porch light, left a lamp on in the living room, and went to bed.

At four o'clock in the morning I woke up. The living room light was still on, and Kyeong Sook was not in her bed.

Gary telephoned her boyfriend's house. The boyfriend's mother answered the phone and said that her son had dropped our daughter off at home about midnight, and that her son was in bed asleep.

A few minutes later the phone rang and it was Kyeong Sook's boyfriend.

"We got into an argument after I brought her home," he reported. His voice dropped to a low whisper. "She was pretty mad. I should have waited until she went into the house, but I didn't. I drove off with her standing on the curb."

When Kyeong Sook was angry, she walked, and she walked fast, usually covering miles, but always before she had returned within a few hours. Our neighborhood is the type where neighbors gossiped together in their bathrobes for a few minutes before bringing in the morning paper. It's the kind of place where UPS parcels can be delivered to your front door step in the morning, and when you come home from work in the evening the package will be sitting there waiting for you. But what if she had been kidnapped right off of our street? Or perhaps she had walked the highway into town and had been abducted?

Gary phoned the police. Terror ripped through my mind. My thoughts raced with horrifying possibilities of what might have happened to her. The police came to our house, and by dawn flyers went up, and her photo was being passed around town. We searched for her, and we talked to all of her friends, and they helped search for her. Neighbors brought us fresh baked bread and pots of soup. The Sunday morning paper ran a story on her disappearance. I wrapped myself in the flannel quilt I had sewn for her when she first arrived from Korea, and waited for the telephone to ring bringing news. There are no words to describe what it is like to have a child go missing.

# ⋛ THE WINTER KYEONG SOOK ⋚
## WENT AWAY, 1995

Eight days later Kyeong Sook breezed into the house, acting as if nothing had happened. Her mouth twisted in a sneer, "I've decided that it's time I move out."

I asked why. Why did she leave? Why on Christmas? Why hadn't she called to let us know she was all right? I asked her where she had been? She offered no explanation. Not then, and not later.

Somehow I hadn't expected it. Her decision was firm. She had already found a place to live, and her plans were already made. There was no doubt about her hardworking nature; she liked her part-time job, and she wanted to begin working full- time. In her mind she was ready, and that was that.

We weren't the best or the worst parents, and we'd done all that we could. I hoped the firm foundation I tried to build on top of her first ten crumbly years would provide her with the skills necessary to live on her own.

"I'm perfectly capable of taking care of myself." Kyeong Sook said. Her body stiffened, and she moved across the room without hesitation and transformed the room into her own inner world. It was a move I knew well. I'd watched her do it at least a million times. It was as if her mind had been colonized. When she was like this there was no way to have a conversation with her. She simply wanted to live on her own, which was a perfectly normal thing for an almost eighteen-year-old to want.

Time with this daughter had run through my fingers like sand. Yet when you only parent a child for eight years before she grows up and goes away, there isn't time for anyone to carry a grudge. You can't wait around to find a good support system, or spend too much time complaining. It's like living with childhood cancer; you can't postpone anything.

But Kyeong Sook's move towards independence was not going to be the fantasy experience I expected: shopping together to buy new bathroom towels, and maybe dishes for a new apartment. Instead she left home abruptly, moved out angry, stuffing everything she owned into green plastic trash bags.

Since she was not yet eighteen, and only a junior in high school, we insisted that she file papers to apply to become an emancipated minor which would grant her the legal status to live on her own as an adult. There were strict stipulations attached to becoming an emancipated minor. She had to be employed, and she must secure a place to live on her own independent from us. She was required to continue with her education and graduate from high school. We contacted Child Protective Services, and since she had never been in trouble with the law, she was allowed to live on her own throughout the filing process. However, she turned eighteen before the court date was set.

In the following months Kyeong Sook sent letters without including a return address, and she refused to see us. Overnight she had become a young woman living on her own. Once I stopped by the department store where she worked, I stayed a distance away so that she wouldn't see me. I watched her standing behind the cash register. I saw a young woman vulnerable, beautiful, off on an incredible flight, arms not to be stopped—a woman strong, terribly strong. She was working at the customer service counter, examining receipts, inspecting returned clothing, counting out cash. It was the same Kyeong Sook I'd known for eight years. There was that certain set to her jaw. Her long black hair was gathered in a ponytail at the nape of her neck, loose strands of hair fell in her face, and she kept tucking them behind one ear, the way I'd watched her do so many times before.

Eventually Kyeong Sook changed jobs. I didn't have her phone number, and I didn't know where she lived. Months passed and then a full year. We tried to act normal, whatever that is. Rather I'd been given a birthmother glimpse—connected to a child, and out of her life. I left plenty of space in the margin, just in case she changed her mind. Violet water still bathed my thoughts; perhaps one day her brain would let all of those sad memories go. At the same time I wondered when my own brain would stop humming hard memories.

In mothering Kyeong Sook I had not let myself feel vulnerable, would not be weak, all in the furtherance of making the family work. So the battle line, which was disguised by necessity, was drawn. Had I been able to ask hard questions our adoption might not have begun to fall apart. But, then again, had I ever been able to ask a hard question, the adoption might never have happened in the first place.

# ≳ THE WINTER VICTOR DIED, 1995 ≲

The telephone rang, and my aunt Dorothy, Victor's mother, was on the other end of the line. "I'll put Victor on," she said.

My cousin spoke mumbled words. "I can't hear you," he complained.

I talked louder and still he could not hear me.

"I love you." I screamed into the receiver. This time he heard me.

"I love you too." His voice was clear.

"I'm lost," I said. "You are still here, but a part of you is gone now. It's the now that we talked about the last time I saw you, while we sat in the car, watching snow slide off the roof of the mortuary."

Four days later my cousin died.

Victor had arranged his own funeral service, down to the tiniest detail of a small white candle for each person. Partly he wanted to save his parents the sorrow of having to make the arrangements, and also because Victor was known for hosting the most eloquent celebrations ever. He wanted his perfectly planned funeral to be his last gift to his friends and family.

The day after his funeral I sat staring at a photograph taken the day we went dog sledding. Victor had a yellow knit scarf around his neck, and it glowed from the photo like a fuzzy golden sun.

## ≳ SPRING, 1996 ≲

In quiet moments late at night I felt twinges of relief that Kyeong Sook was no longer living with us. I was glad to be away from her constant mood swings. When she left she packed those emotional highs and lows and took them with her. My sense of being freed made me feel like the worst mother in the world.

If only I'd realized at the time what I was feeling was normal. Back then I didn't know it was OK for a mother to feel both sad and a bit relieved when her daughter moved out on her own. I didn't have enough life experience to understand that adoptive mothers and adoptive daughters who had a rough transition bonding together in the beginning of their union, naturally had equally tough times separating when the child began to reach adulthood. And since I didn't know any of this back then, guilt locked onto me. It left footprints on my soul. I tried to out walk it, write past it, sleep it off.

It was impossible to sleep for more than three hours without waking up. The sound of an owl pressed against the night. When I finally did fall asleep, in my dreams water poured from a house on a hill, and an old woman named Heaven lived inside. Night after night in my dreams I climbed the hill to meet her.

Months passed. I was still in awful shape when the phone rang. My friend Annie was on the other end of the line.

"Sure, I'll drive to New Mexico with you," I told her.

Whenever he could, Gary managed to get away for two or three day fishing trips. Yet only once since Jay developed a brain tumor had I taken a break and gone off on my own without Gary and the children. I was way overdue for some time away. The plan was for me to drive to Santa Fe with Annie, and while she attended a conference I would stay with my friend Chris who lived in a rural area north of town.

Gary was slicing onions and turned, facing me, grinning, "A weekend of contrasts is what you are going to find."

"Annie has an earthy side to her." I giggled. "She will probably wear jeans and shoes with a little heel." I opened a hamburger bun and spread mustard on both sides and tried to imagine my friends meeting each other for the first time. Chris with waist-length hair tied back in ponytail, with muddy boots. Annie would greet him with a tiny hand, smooth, oval painted nails wearing her grand-mother's platinum ring glistening with diamonds.

"Annie was wondering what clothes to pack." I passed the jar of mustard to Gary. "I told her not to be surprised if I came back on Sunday wearing the same jeans and flannel shirt I started out in."

The thing I treasured about my twenty-five-year friendship with Chris was how it kept me honest. When I told him some-thing, I knew right away if I was lying to myself, and I could tell that he knew, too. But this time I was all talked out. Mostly Chris preferred to be quiet, too, which was why he was the perfect friend for me to spend the weekend with.

Annie dropped me off in the evening as the sun began to set. When I arrived Chris was in the middle of reading a book. I was tired from the long drive, and I could tell he was tired from his day.

The first thing I did was lie down on the couch and kick off my shoes. We chatted for a few minutes, and then I fell asleep. When I woke up I noticed that Chris had taken off his hat, and his gray hair lay flattened in several directions. Two times he raised his eyes from the book he was reading and glanced over at me. I could anticipate his mood by watching his face; he was enjoying a quiet evening.

I got my book, and put my bare feet on the wooly brown goatskin on the floor. In the fireplace, flames leaped up and shadows began to slope across the wall. The room smelled of wet adobe plaster and the cured scent of old hides. We read until the last log of the night burned down, and the fire fell to pieces. I appreciated the fact that I was not obligated to make small talk, and I soaked up every moment of the silence and peace that filled the room.

"It's going to be cold tonight," Chris said handing me a sleeping bag.

"Can I borrow a T-Shirt?" I asked.

"Over there," he said, pointing at a pile of clothes in a plastic basket on the floor.

"Good night," he said and he crawled through the low doorway up the stairs. I listened to his footsteps fade away on the clanking boards, then slipped off my jeans, and pulled a navy blue, long-sleeved shirt out of the stack. I opened the window wide so I could see stars falling across the night sky. The sleeping bag smelled of wood smoke and sun-baked corduroy, like pitch from juniper wood; it smelled like Chris. The shirt was big on me. I curled my legs and folded the shirt around my knees, and pulled the sleeping bag up around my chin. Fireflies flew in the open window and wildly darted around the room—clear white beads of light shimmering, flashing, and glowing in the air. I lay silent and felt their current flowing into me. The tension in the muscles of my shoulders unwound with each breath I took.

We filled the next day with a hike in the arroyo and more reading by the fire, and by Sunday morning when it was time to meet Annie and drive home, I was relaxed.

# ⟩ FALL, 1996 ⟨

Jay was in remission and the brain tumor was gone. Each time he had an MRI, the scan came back perfectly clear. He was back to snorkeling at the beach, and he looked healthy, if fragile. I was supposed to be happy, and I was happy; but I still had terrible moments of despair over Kyeong Sook, and Jay's fifth-year, post-cancer well-check appointment left me feeling like I'd stepped into a shooting gallery.

Our insurance company, a California HMO, decided that Jay didn't need to see an oncologist anymore. He was routed to a general practice pediatrician. Luck held; the doctor assigned was one of the best in town. I told the new doctor what I knew, recounting our past five years, my vocabulary automatically carrying perfect medical jargon.

The world of childhood cancer taught me to speak professional-to-professional, to shake off the happily-ever-after aspect of life. I wanted to be told the brutal facts, yet even the slightest emotion in my voice sometimes prevented doctors from telling me everything I wanted to know. We were not out of the woods yet.

When Jay asked to be excused to go to the bathroom, the doctor raised his head and turned to me; he shifted the weight of his upper body, "Think of your son as having had the same amount of radiation as the Hiroshima survivors; he's at a high risk for developing leukemia." I tensed and tightened my toes. I knew secondary cancers were common, yet it was one of those things I tried not to think about.

"It's a recurring type of brain tumor," I said. "Most of the time it comes back."

The doctor looked straight into my eyes. "So you understand what we're dealing with then."

"Quite frankly your boy is making excellent progress." The doctor patted my arm, "But I'm worried about his eyes. Has his left eye always turned in like that?"

The news that Jay needed eye surgery hit hard. The medical name given for the procedure was: Strabismus repair OU. I had to sign forms saying I was aware of the risks: potential loss of the eye, loss of vision, infection and bleeding. The diagnosis was hypertropia exotropia amblyopia. It meant Jay's eyes weren't working well together. He did most of his seeing out of one eye, probably a result of all of the radiation.

I was not eager to fix this problem. Jay seemed to be getting by fine. After the brain tumor had been removed, Jay had begun closing one eye when reading. His team of doctor's felt it was eye muscle damage resulting from the tumor. Jay didn't mind keeping one eye shut when he read, but I hoped he might discover a whole new world of easy vision, which would justify putting him through yet another surgical procedure.

The pediatric ophthalmology waiting room was filled with children and parents. The other mothers and fathers looked as tense as I felt. I kept wishing myself back to our syndactyly release surgery days, a time when I was a medically innocent mother supporting Jay through routine surgeries to separate his fingers. Back then I only felt that we had a few small hills to climb. This time I was desperately afraid.

The night before surgery we were given instructions. It was a familiar routine. Nothing to eat or drink after midnight. Don't forget to bring your insurance card. Then the heart statement, "He may be a bit too old for this, but if he has a special toy, we will be glad to keep it with him during the procedure."

Jay was nearly thirteen. Would he want to bring Small Bear? The teddy bear had been with him for all five syndactyly release surgeries, for the brain tumor surgery and for both of his shunt insertion procedures. As a young child Jay tenderly cared for his stuffed animals. His teddy bear wore his sister's doll sweaters; he wrapped him in the doll sized flannel quilt hand-made by me, and he gave him a bottle of pretend milk to drink.

Originally Small Bear had a windup key music box inside him. When Jay was in kindergarten the music quit playing. One afternoon, with Jay at my side, I made a small slit in the fuzzy brown material and lifted out the broken music box. I pulled out handfuls of matted mildew smelling batting, and then I washed Small Bear's limp puppet-like body. We hung him on the clothesline to dry, and then I put new batting inside him and stitched him up. If Jay didn't want Small Bear with him this time, I thought I might like to keep the teddy bear with me.

As big as he was, Jay tucked his teddy bear under his arm and off he went.

The surgery was successful. I breathed a sigh of relief. A week later Jay's eyes were still blood red, but all was well physically, the procedure went perfectly. Emotionally he was withdrawn. This non-cancer-related surgery unearthed memories from brain tumor surgery. If you left Jay alone he would come to you when he was ready to talk. If you pushed him into talking he was hair-triggered.

Jealous feelings from Jay's numerous surgeries, from the cancer days, resurfaced in Vanessa. Her anger was so unexpected. At age fifteen she was warm, understanding and swept along by a dark storm of emotions. From the couch where she sat curled up, swaddled in an afghan, her voice was passionate and loud. "It's not fair. Every time Jay has surgery nobody does anything special for me."

Busy with my own thin, worn endurance, at first I grumbled, and then caught myself. I sat down beside her and let her rage. The air around her vibrated. Her anger was wholly that of the ten-year-old girl she was when her brother suddenly developed a brain tumor. She let fury fly for almost ten minutes, and then she let her head fall against my shoulder.

# ⊰ SPRING, 1997 ⊱

For the past year we hadn't attended any of the childhood cancer survivor support group meetings. I decided to become active again, and I also began volunteering for the Veteran Parent Program within We Can—Pediatric Brain Tumor Network. It was my turn to give back and support those parents with children who had been recently diagnosed. Veteran parents served as examples of families who had been there and survived the ordeal. But even after six years, as I met with parents at the hospital and listened to them talk, I felt returned to newly diagnosed status. Looking at these parents was like looking into a mirror at myself. My fears returned.

Within days I discovered loose hairs falling from my head. For weeks I gathered up the thirteen-inch-long strands of fallen hair that collected on our wood floor and then wound around my toes. I decided to stop brushing my hair inside the house. Instead, I brushed in my garden and let those fallen hairs blow in the wind, winding around the branches of a peach tree. Maybe a bird would weave my hairs into her nest.

Strikingly handsome weeds grew at the edge of my garden. It was a dry, sparse garden; a manageable ten-by-eight plot stretching along the backyard fence line that bordered the creek and its surrounding wilderness. Zinnias and cosmos grew alongside wild snapdragons and hummingbird sage. A birdfeeder stood in the middle, atop a ten-foot-tall pole. Below the feeder, birdseed sprouted in a crazy tangle of wheat-like stalks, along with deep-apricot milkweed blossoms. You couldn't plan to grow a garden like mine, certainly not in the city. You had to be willing to embrace what nature offered. A flock of ravens gossiped harshly at me. Red-heart mountain lilac, thick, leathery, and shiny, tossed and bent in the wind. And hair collected in my brush. A few more fell to the ground or floated away in the wind. Standing in my garden while I brushed my hair became a beloved ritual.

One morning I noticed that my hair was no longer falling out. My hands reached out and pulled the brush through my hair in rapid strokes, but only three single hairs were released. Ten or fifteen minutes each morning in my garden had soothed me, gave me calm. My tension dropped away. We were managing the shifting complications of raising a son who was a brain tumor survivor. I felt an inner strength rising. Knowing after managing to come this far I would be able to meet any challenge that might lay ahead.

In the long term, it was clear that being able to revisit my emotions, and then finish working through them, made me a stronger support to other parents of children with brain tumors.

I had not yet made such gains as a veteran adoptive parent. I was still suffering deeply the pain of being the mother of an estranged daughter, and what felt to me like a failed adoption. It was as if I had somehow failed. Occasionally I ran into someone who had been in contact with Kyeong Sook. The gossip circulating through town reported that she was happy. She was setting her own standards and focusing on her potential, not her problems.

Many people believe a lot of things that aren't true about those of us who choose transracial adoption and adopt older kids. We don't have the subtle art of parenting perfected; we're ordinary parents, the ones who manage, with more or less grace, to learn the new parenthood lessons that must be learned. You need passion to adopt a half-grown child. It's an experience unpredictable, unpretentious, rich, sometimes shattering, and profound.

The adoption agency had carefully evaluated our family for strengths. We didn't have any serious marital difficulties. We didn't have unrealistic expectations for our children's success (other than believing that no child is so damaged by past happenings that he cannot eventually learn to trust).

We must have reflected the ability to provide an older child with permanence, our household being a place to truly experience family. We liked children and enjoyed the challenge of parenting; most importantly, we knew kids didn't say thank you. We were verbally bright, well read, and without a shred of practical experience to prepare us for what came.

We adopted a ten-year-old, our third child, our second adoption. Adopting transracially made a small impact on me compared to the larger impact of becoming the mother of a child so neglected and shuffled between so many homes that she contained the rage and sadness that defined her childhood. The side effects of abuse are pretty much the same within every race and culture. How different would our lives have been if someone had prepared me for this?

What if someone in Korea had thought to ask Kyeong Sook if she wanted to be adopted *before* she was sent to the United States? After she was placed in our family a therapist did ask her.

She said, "No, not really. I didn't want a new family, but nobody listened to me."

Clearly she needed a family. Our photograph albums show eight years of smiles at birthday parties, family vacations, but in each photo I look at her face and wonder what she was feeling. We had moments of happiness, days even, yet our years together were mostly a push-pull of subtle pressures and sudden knocks. There was some kind of barrier we couldn't break through. Yet she blossomed outside our family with outside relationships. She was happiest when a girlfriend extended an overnight invitation. She was the perfect houseguest; other parents adored her. Then she felt witnessed as a person.

Over the years we found that the minute we said "international adoption," the door was closed to us for most provisions of general child welfare support services. For example we could have asked for a Safety Net Clause providing some financial help during the time period when anger made her a danger to herself, when she truly needed a temporary respite from us. If we'd had more support maybe she would not have felt so desperate to run away.

Instead we toughened it out, and our other children suffered greatly; we could have been better parents to them if we'd had more help for Kyeong Sook.

It helped a great deal when my friend told me a story about his adult son who had always done wonderfully as a child when he was away from home visiting friends or relatives, and that he always did less well at home. Even now that his son was nearly thirty, it was the same thing. My friend smiled and said, "This is good because that's where my son will be spending the rest of his life—out in the adult world."

Of course a Korean family in Korea would have been an ideal match for Kyeong Sook. It would have been even better if her situation within her birth family had been one which she could have stayed and thrived in. Instead she was sent to me in the United States.

I couldn't give her the family she longed for, but if belonging is a launching pad for becoming, I could breath a sigh of relief. Kyeong Sook always did do well out in the world.

## ≥ SUMMER, 1998 ≤

The plane rumbled down the runway into Kimpo International Airport. My heart was jumping. Jay and I were in Korea and I was so excited I could hardly breath. Jay had received a scholarship to travel to Korea and participate in the Friends of Korea Family Exchange Program. We were on our way along with nine other adoptive families.

As we stepped out of the plane, the humid July air turned into sweat that ran down my face. I watched Jay. He stood next to me, fourteen years old, beaming, wearing stonewashed jeans, a navy blue polo shirt and new tennis shoes. He stopped to mop the sweat off his forehead and turned sideways to cast a glance at me. I could see my white face reflected in his black-brown eyes. A swarm of people pushed past us, moving us along at a clipping pace.

"If we get separated go to the baggage claim area," I said. Jay gave me an odd look and said, "Don't worry, Mom. Do you realize what you look like? Everybody is Korean, I could spot you from a mile away."

Outside the airport a chartered bus awaited. Our group of children and parents had chatted together nonstop getting to know each other during the long journey from San Francisco to Seoul. Now, on the bus that would take us to Chonan to meet our host families we rode silently, listening and watching. Our bus ride took us past streets teeming with well-dressed people. The air hummed with activity, horns honking above the roar of traffic, and cars grinding gears, the sounds gathering intensity.

"Seoul looks exactly like Koreatown in Los Angeles," Jay mused. "It's almost the same as San Francisco too, only everything is so Korean-looking." Skyscrapers, posh hotels and restaurants, classy designer shops, fast food, and expensive cars lined the streets, with everything written in Hangul. We left the metropolitan area, and the traffic on the freeway was at a standstill. Our bus zoomed in the diamond lane, passing hundreds of cars stuck in traffic, and dropped us off in Chonan at the youth center where our host families waited to greet us.

The group of Korean families stood in a cluster, laughing and talking with each other. I listened to the sound of the words without understanding their meaning. Friendly voices. Still we were pretty nervous, since all we knew about our host families was information provided on a two-page questionnaire, and they knew equally as little about us. One by one we were each introduced; everyone bowed and smiled. The midsummer sun blasted down on us, and a hot wind made Jay's black hair stand up straight. All around, the air simmered heavy with the scent of crushed garlic and sesame. Then our host family squeezed our luggage into their compact car and off we went.

THE SUMMER OF 1998, ACCORDING to the neighbors in Chonan, was the hottest in recent memory. Our host family included a mom, dad and their young sons. The mother, Mee Hyang, who was well dressed, slim and petite with curly, short, dark hair, didn't speak English. I guessed myself to be about fifteen years her senior. Immediately we both picked up on the fact that we were exactly the same height and about the same weight.

The children, nine-year-old Young Oh and seven-year-old Soo Myoung didn't speak English either. The day we arrived, the father was on a business trip. Thirty seconds into our visit the neighbor women began to arrive, all with children in tow. Round-faced women, apron-bound, carried pots of ice-cold *shikye* sweet rice drink, platters of *pindaettok* mung bean pancakes garnished with green leaves of chrysanthemum and red pepper slices. We were in a tenth floor apartment, large, three bedrooms, two bathrooms, spotlessly clean. A china closet gleamed in the corner, framed oil paintings on the wall, potted plants, books on shelves, high-tech stereo equipment, a computer, fax machine, and a large fish aquarium.

Low tables were pulled out, one for the children and another for the women. We sat cross-legged on the floor. The meal was communal with all of us dipping our chopsticks into the same bowl of *kimchi*. After we finished eating, over at the kids' table, I watched Jay throwing himself into a game of Mancala. Undaunted, Jay taught the group how to play the game. We brought the Mancala game as a gift to our host family, and immediately it was a huge success. The children, communicating only in grunts and shrieks, played for hours. The afternoon sunlight glimmered from the window and changed from goldenrod to a rosy red sunset while the neighbor women laughed and chatted. I smiled and nodded my head. This was partly to draw attention away from my lack of verbal abilities. After two years of Korean language school I knew only nouns and verbs. There were benefits, I'd discovered, of abstaining from speech. It gave me time to draw in the raw powerful language that flowed so freely from these women.

That evening we were taken out to dinner. The Korean restaurant was posh and formal, with black leather, upholstered chairs, tables covered in crisp, white linen, set with china and silver chopsticks. A large crowd of people, including most of the neighbors, had been invited. The woman who had arranged the dinner had lived in Chicago for ten years and spoke fluent English. Her father owned the restaurant and had treated us to this ultra-expensive meal of rich, rich exquisite foods. When it was time to leave, I thanked our host, a man in his mid-seventies who was dressed in a trendy suit with an expensive gold watch glimmering on his wrist.

"Thank you," I said in Korean. Then because I wanted to let him know how much I appreciated his kindness, speaking in Korean I continued by saying, "Thank you for a delightful time." The man's face turned pink, there was a twinkle in his eye, and he looked like he wanted to smile but he held his expression straight. I strolled outside into the balmy night air, feeling proud of my rapidly developing Korean language skills.

Outside the restaurant, the man's daughter, who was about my age, grabbed my arm. "Don't ever say that again," she said in English.

"What did I do wrong?"

"You thanked my father in a way that suggested you were thanking him for sexual favors."

She grabbed my hand, and linked her arm through mine as we walked towards the car. Then she began to giggle with her hand covering her mouth, and then I started to giggle a little myself.

Around midnight somebody pulled out a Korean-English dictionary, and I was able to grasp that the plan was to wake up in time for an early morning hike, then go to the bathhouse. I'd never been to a Korean bathhouse, and I loved hiking. I drifted off to sleep looking forward to the morning.

Instead I woke up in the middle of the night with a stomach-ache. By seven a.m. I was worse, and called for Jay.

"Get the Korean dictionary and look up the word for illness, and go get Young Oh's mother. Just say *Ohma*, and point to the word that means sick."

I fell asleep and opened my eyes to see many black-haired, high-cheeked women standing over me. It was noon; my skin was grayish.

"You go doctor," one of the women said in English.

"I'll be better in a little while." I argued. I pushed the skin on my leg, and it dented like it was made out of clay.

"Okay, doctor." I agreed.

The neighborhood clinic was new and modern, spotlessly clean with a Korean-style squatter toilet. I sank to my knees and vomited again. The doctor didn't speak English. A woman translated for him: the diagnosis was food poisoning, probably from eating at an American style fast food hamburger chain the day before in Seoul.

"You get shot with needle," she translated next.

"No needle," I insisted. I felt in control. I was sick, but didn't feel overly worried; I'd taken Imodium, the diarrhea had stopped.

"Little needle, not big one," she reported. "Not hurt."

"Let me see the needle," I demanded. Then because I didn't know how else to phrase it I requested a fresh needle, using the word "fresh" in a way that was meant to be spoken at the green grocer's to ask for fresh vegetables. The doctor brought out a package of unopened, sterilized needles and a new IV bag containing liquid to replace the body fluids I'd lost. He held it up for me to see, the ingredients were listed in English.

"You better fast," the doctor explained.

"Okay," I agreed and held out my arm. The smell of alcohol drifted over me. The neighbor women gathered around me,

"We go home, come back in one hour."

Jay flashed me a worried look.

"I'll be fine," I announced, and then off they all went.

An air conditioner hummed in the corner. Outside it was 105, not counting the waves of heat from the pavement. Inside the clinic, cool air blasted around me. My head rested on a green quilted pillowcase. A small voice in my mind kept saying, maybe I ought to be worried. But I didn't feel worried. I was amused.

For years I had wanted to bring Jay to Korea, but I was afraid to because something might go wrong with his shunt, and then he would need to be hospitalized. Even though he was seven years past a brain tumor, Jay still had a shunt because hydrocephalus persisted. Shunts are such tricky things; like the plumbing in a house they can block and back up or malfunction. Yet here we were in Korea, and *I* was in the hospital. Instead of feeling worried I felt confident I was receiving care equal to, and probably better than that of many medical clinics at home in America, so I closed my eyes and went to sleep.

An hour later Young Oh's mother and her neighbor friends came to get me as promised.

"We go to museums now," one of the women said. The doctor told her to make sure they gave me plenty of water and Gatorade to drink.

Jay pressed his face next to mine, and whispered, "Do we have to go to museums?"

Even though I was feeling a lot better, I explained to the women that I was still much too weak for an afternoon of walking, so we piled together in the car and went home.

The night before I'd slept in the youngest son's bedroom, in a twin bed. Now I was invited to rest in the master bedroom, on the queen sized *tol ch'im dae*, a stone bed. It had a wood carved head and footboard and instead of a mattress, the sleeping surface was a polished stone slab, expensive looking, beautiful and hard. After about twenty minutes of resting on this bed, I went into the living room and spent the rest of the afternoon relaxing on the floor.

Rather than holding us apart, my sick day actually strengthened bonds. We were able to share stay-at-home time with our host family in a way that probably wouldn't have happened if I were feeling healthy. With help from the Korean-English dictionary I asked Young Oh's mother if she liked swimming or camping. At first she said *ahn chu an hey yo* which is a polite way to say she didn't care for either.

But I pressed her further; finally she giggled and said the Korean word that meant she hated swimming and camping.

I pointed to myself and said that I liked both. Young Oh's mother fell into the game.

"Indoor girl," she said pointing to herself. "Outdoor girl," she said pointing to me. We laughed. Jay looked up the Korean word for fisherman and pointed to himself. There were moments of real intimacy between us. We had time to rest and shore up. I was fed homey Korean comfort foods, soothing creamed rice dishes, with cucumber *kimchi* on the side of course. I discovered Mee Hwang delighted in inviting friends over and treating them with her home cooked food. In the neighborhood just the mention of her name made everyone think of her delicious meals.

"Sometimes when I smell rice cooking, and everybody is singing in Korean, I can almost remember being a baby in Korea," Jay admitted. "It's not a regular memory I can think about as long as I want. It's much quicker than that."

At fourteen, Jay was delighted to play big brother to the younger kids. Making paper airplanes and an afternoon of watching Korean cartoons were simple things that still warmed Jay's heart. The kids pulled board games out of the closet, and by the time Mr. Lee came home from his business trip, the whole house was warm with our day together. Or maybe it was the *kimchi tchigae* simmering on the stove. Whatever, it was awfully nice.

In the morning I woke up totally refreshed. We climbed out of our beds early. Breakfast was a rice porridge known as *chuk* garnished with pine nuts and toasted seaweed. It's my favorite Korean breakfast food, and it tasted especially good to me after having been sick.

We piled onto a bus with the combined group of American and Korean families in the Friends of Korea Family Exchange Program and headed for Korean Boy and Girl Scout Camp. The bus dropped us off at Taechon Beach where we spent the day body surfing Korean waves.

That evening around a campfire we did the usual type of Boy and Girl Scout activities. First the Korean families put on a skit portraying traditional Korean life ways. Then they did a modern day comedy skit. Next the American families were asked to present an activity. For our contribution first I read the book "Everybody needs a Rock" by Byrd Baylor in English. Then Young Oh's mother read the story translated into Korean. While everyone sat in a circle around the fire, Jay passed around a basket filled with tiny stones, and each person selected a rock to keep as their very own. Later a Korean man who was an elder in the community came to me. He pulled out a hankie and dabbed at his eyes, and then he cleared his throat.

"When I was a boy growing up in Korea," he said, "I always carried a special rock with me." His voice quavered when he spoke. He ran his fingers over the smooth, round stone, and then he tucked it into his pocket.

The next morning all of the Americans, including parents, were given *chongo* drum lessons. We each sat on the floor with our own drum and for over an hour we followed along with the instructor and beat out a rhythm, not quite in unison. After that jam-packed week filled with activity, Jay and I said goodbye to the Lee family and left to go back to Seoul with our group of adoptive families.

We were not on a typical tour where everyone in the group was expected to stay together. Once we were in Seoul we were able to break up into smaller groups to do whatever we wanted, according to our interests. While staying with the Lee family, our days and nights were tightly scheduled and predictable. Everything was arranged for us with translators on hand. Choices were made for us, and no one ever asked us to give an opinion. We barely needed to think on our own at all. Our biggest challenge was to keep up the fast pace.

Once we were in Seoul, however, and on our own, everything was unpredictable. We stayed in a modestly priced hotel in an all-Korean speaking neighborhood. We pulled out our English/Korean dictionaries and did the best we could to communicate, since nearly everyone we came into contact with did not speak any English.

We were typical tourists. The first day, along with a group of four others, we headed for Dongdaemun Market, in the old market area. People squeezed past us on the sidewalk. The heavy, hot summer air was pungent with the smell of sesame, ginger and the perspiration of many people crowded together wilting in the hot sun. The sidewalks and alleyways were jammed with baskets stuffed with fresh produce, and pink and yellow plastic tubs were filled with fish. There were shoes for sale, power tools, leather goods, and fake designer purses lined the walkways. Jay, a black-belt shopper, purchased a couple of CDs from a sidewalk shop where Korean pop music blared from large speakers. He became good at asking the question, "How much does this cost?" in Korean. Usually he managed to get a good discount.

Next we scoped out the other section in the southern area known as the New Market where there are modern shopping malls. By now our confidence picked up, and we parents allowed our teenaged kids to go off on their own. We wanted them to have an opportunity to discover what it felt like to be in Seoul without white parents in tow.

Jay said he didn't feel at all shy. Though it was obvious he was an adoptee and an American-raised Korean, Jay said everyone he met warmed right up to him. Within a short amount of time he learned to speak quite a bit of Korean. He was easily able to communicate in stores and restaurants.

It was clear Jay was beginning to answer the question, "What would it be like to live in Korea?" He walked as if his feet grew up from the ground. I could tell he felt a connection to the land that formed him, carved the high bones in his face.

Jay wanted to go to the DMZ. We climbed through the tunnels that snake their way to North Korea where he came face to face with a very young North Korean soldier standing guard.

The day trips to Kapsa and Donghaksa Buddhist temples lodged in my mind, and to this day whenever I close my eyes and remember back and nurture the moment, I can still hear the sound of cicadas, and feel the warm humid air surround me as I walk the long path to the temple.

Near the end of our stay in Korea, Jay and I, along with three other adoptive families and their teenaged children, went to Holt. It's the agency in Korea through which Jay had been adopted. Our appointment was scheduled for noon. We entered through the medical clinic waiting area entrance; the same small room where Jay had received well baby check-ups when he was placed in the custody of Holt.

The assistant director greeted us, and then each family was led off separately to meet with a social worker. The circumstances surrounding Jay's departure from Korea and his arrival in America was far beyond the average experience. Holt in Korea played a central role in this. When Gary and I went to the Holt office in California, in 1984 to sign acceptance documents necessary for a child born with special medical problems, we met another couple also there to sign adoption acceptance papers.

At first we thought an error was made. The documents for both children had the same medical diagnosis—syndactyly. Then we discovered what we thought was a second error. Both sets of documents had the name Gary as the adoptive father's first name. Within minutes we realized this was not a mistake. The couple we met, Gary and Margaret Richardson, was also adopting a baby with syndactyly. They were days away from traveling to Korea to receive their new daughter. The Richardson's offered to hand-carry our documents to Korea with them. This was long before fax machines were used. In those days everything had to be mailed or hand-carried to Korea.

"If Holt will let us, we will be happy to bring your son back with us." Gary Richardson offered. It was a fun thought yet it seemed highly unlikely.

A week later on December 10, 1984, we received a phone call from Holt in Seoul asking for our permission to let Gary and Margaret escort Jay to America. The next day we met the Richardsons at the airport, and they placed Jay in my arms. When we got home we telephoned the Holt office in California and let them know our baby arrived from Korea. Holt in California had no idea, and they were stunned with surprise. We began what turned out to be a life-long friendship with the Richardson family. They had a daughter the same age as our daughter Vanessa. Jay and their daughter Lynne had traveled to America on the same flight, and they both had syndactyly. By our conversation with the Korean social worker, it was apparent this story was recorded in Jay's adoption file.

I knew Jay had great expectations of having his adoption files read to him and hearing the words, "What would you like to know about your past?"

It didn't happen. The file was placed in his lap, and it contained only the original documents that we already had copies of at home. I knew Jay was hoping that the file would list the names of his birth-parents. But the only piece of new information was a small photo taken when he was about four or five months. Jay was brighteyed, wearing light blue pajamas, with bare toes wiggling, and lying on a yellow *yo* (blanket) with a little name tag in the corner that said his name, "Jhun, Kook Yung" in Korean.

"Is it OK if I keep the photo?" Jay asked. It was the first photograph we had seen of him when he was a baby, less than a year old.

The Holt staff paid careful attention to Jay. He was led down a hall way, and he returned a few minutes wearing a lime green and pink Hanbok. His arms were loaded with gifts for me as well. Jay and I handed out the gifts we brought along for the Holt staff.

After our separate meetings ended, all the adoptive families gathered and were all treated to a lunch of cold noodle soup, four different types of *kimchi*, and about a dozen other side dishes.

We spent the rest of the day playing with and caring for babies at the Holt Reception Center. These babies were in process of getting ready to leave Korea and be adopted in the United States. We sat on the floor in the same room where Jay and Lynne had once stayed while they were in the process of being adopted.

Rows and rows of baby cribs lined the walls. They were not new cribs, and I tried to imagine which crib Jay might have been in when he was here. For over an hour Jay sat on a *yo* on the floor with a baby boy gathered against him, sleeping cradled in his arms. Both of them were so beautiful I couldn't take my eyes off of them.

That night, though it was not planned, Jay was on the telephone talking with someone who knew his birthmother. It turned out that Mr. Lee, the father of the family we stayed with in Chonan, had grown up in the same small rural town where Jay was born, and Mr. Lee's father was a retired chief of police. He had promised Jay that he would make a few phone calls to see if anyone in town had any information on his birth family.

My heart thumped. I took deep, slow breaths, and my hands clenched themselves. The minutes ticked away, and then Jay dropped the telephone receiver back into its cradle. I glanced up at him. His eyes rested on the phone. I waited.

"He said he thinks it's best if I don't try to contact her." Jay's voice was rough, as if the words scraped his throat. I could tell that for the first time the facts surrounding his adoption completely rocked his security; meaning the syndactyly; the fingers on both of his hands that were fused together when he was born. After we adopted Jay, all ten of his fingers had been surgically separated, but as a baby in Korea, Jay's hands had resembled tiny mittens.

I watch my son straighten his shoulders, take a deep breath, hold his head high, but his dark eyes, swelling with moisture, were not afraid to look into mine. Then he settled back into the chair, as if that ended the matter. I felt caught inside a miniature world where everything is frozen in place like a scene inside a glass paperweight. I stood inside this glass world, looking out at my son.

Jay sat beside me. The sides of our legs touched very slightly. "If your birthmother does not want to meet you, it's not because of anything you've done," I said. "It took a great deal of courage and sadness for her to let you go," I told Jay. An expression of interest crossed his face. He looked at me with his huge moonbeam eyes.

We sat side-by-side trying to imagine the day he was born; his *ohm-mah* breathing him in, trying to remember the way he smelled. Maybe she carried him on her back in a quilted, maroon, piggyback blanket. As we combed through our imagined details of the day, my heart tipped as I watched Jay. At how he was able to throw himself back into life without crowding the pain. That's one thing he learned from a cancer diagnosis; to do things in their proper times. Better to go through it now, while the feelings were fresh.

Still, getting close to finding his birthmother then having to pull back left a great hole for Jay. After a few more phone calls we left a message including our home telephone number, in case his birth family decided to contact him.

Next we scheduled a visit to Sun Rak Won, the orphanage where Jay lived for the first year of his life prior to Holt. At Sun Rak Won, Jay had shared a small room with two other baby boys. One of the babies was missing a left ear. The other had a cleft palate, and Jay had syndactyly. The social worker responsible for matching Jay with our family was kind enough to show us photos of all three babies together, and she relayed stories the staff at Sun Rak Won told her. It was the only thread Jay had leading to his past. Going back to Sun Rak Won was important to him.

But when we woke up the next morning, monsoon rains pounded down heavily. The rain continued all week and brought the plan to a sudden halt. Staying on the trail would have meant asking the Lee's to drive us many miles to Sun Rak Won in pouring rain and in heavy traffic. So, instead of talking the Lee's into taking us, I talked Jay out of going, saying we would return to Korea next year, and we would go to his orphanage then. I stood in the doorway of the hotel and watched the rain coming down hard on the sidewalk. A blowing rain was beginning to soak through my shirt, and if I had it to do over again I would've insisted on making the journey to Sun Rak Won.

# ⇝ FALL, 1998 ⇜

I followed Jay into the bathroom; he opened the medicine cabinet and reached for the bottle of Advil.

"Do you have a headache again?" I asked.

He shrugged his shoulders, then hiccupped hard, and ducked his head in the toilet and threw up. He wretched until his stomach heaved in frantic dry spasms. Tears welled in Jay's eyes. For the past two days he had been having headaches off and on. I sank into the deep, silent panic that made me calm. I knew the tumor was back.

Our primary care physician called in an authorization for an MRI. Jay hid the fear he felt behind a mask of quiet strength. It was the week before Thanksgiving, ten days before his fifteenth birthday.

Each day, as often as I could, I kept my eyes on Jay. I memorized his every move. I watched him talk on the phone with friends, snuck side-glances while he did his homework, as he sprinted out the door to go to school. In the middle of the night I poked my head into his room, and I could hear him hiccupping, steady, quiet hiccups that didn't interrupt his sleep.

That week Jay was elected student of the month, and he got a lead part in the school play. My idyll of familyhood continued until the MRI confirmed my worst fear—the tumor was back, an anaplastic ependymoma, and this time its fingers spread into the brainstem.

We had to decide on a plan of treatment. We contacted the surgeon who had preformed Jay's first brain tumor surgery. Surgery was scheduled.

Luck held, most of the tumor was successfully resected. In less than a week Jay was out of the hospital, recovering well. But what to do about the remaining brain tumor slivers that were inoperable? He had *already* received his lifetime dose of whole brain radiation, and the chemotherapy drugs he used with the first diagnosis offered little hope of curing a recurrent tumor. There was a small chance that stereotactic radio surgery might be of some help in stalling tumor growth. We set up a consultation and began the initial treatment plan.


ON CHRISTMAS EVE A LARGE BOX filled with One Thousand Paper Cranes arrived in the mail. Good Luck Cranes. Susan, a friend of Jay's, made a plea to all of her friends, and posted a notice on an origami website, to fold paper cranes for Jay. She enclosed the original envelopes the paper cranes had arrived in. The postmarks were from all over the US along with a handful from Denmark, Holland, Korea, and Germany.

The paper birds arrived folded flat, pre-strung, and ready to hang. We had golden cranes, fancy green paper with pink parasols on it. Cranes made in brilliant blues, yellow, and orange. A few of the cranes were folded with cherry blossom paper, and some were bright green neon cranes. Some were folded from newsprint, and others were glow-in-the dark cranes. Twenty cranes made from paper with tiny Korean flags. Crimson, purple and magenta, a rainbow of paper cranes. A Japanese legend about the crane tells that it is suppose to live for a thousand years, and if a sick person folds one thousand paper cranes, the gods will grant his wish and make him healthy again.

As we unfolded each tiny wing, and strung the paper cranes from a skinny oak branch we could feel a thousand good wishes encircle Jay. Each paper crane was a loving tribute. We could feel the power, the precision and devotion in the folding, the unfolding of each wing, a prayer.

I encouraged Jay and Vanessa to continue on with their ordinary routines, to live as normally as possible. Someone from the PTA at Jay's school called and wanted me to contribute a dessert for a bake sale. I didn't tell her Jay had a brain tumor; instead I agreed to bake cookies. Normally Jay rose to our household dessert challenges. He enjoyed cooking and baking. He got out the baking sheets, the eggs and measured out the flour, and then from a rocking chair he directed my efforts to produce his perfected chocolate chip cookie recipe. I placed three cookies in each plastic bag tied with purple ribbons and delivered them to the bake sale. I felt like I was on some kind of an emotional layaway plan: experience life now and feel it later.


MY FRIENDSHIP WITH AHRYUN had stood the test of time. We maintained regular contact and talked frequently. She was still living in Sweden. The only time I let my fears surface was in my conversations with Ahryun. Most of the time I forced myself to stay in the moment, and didn't allow myself the luxury of worrying about the future. A future without Jay in it was impossible to imagine.

I watched Jay thumb through the newspaper. "So why do you suppose when a person dies from cancer they say he lost the battle?" Jay questioned. His face was pinched with confusion. "Don't worry Mom, I know dying is not about losing." And with the zeal of a kid determined to restore order to the universe he announced, "Heaven is filled with winners."

Having a positive attitude was important to Jay. Although he had very low energy he attended school half-day because he loved school. He helped his friends understand that it's important not to think of cancer in terms of "fighting it," or "beating it back." You don't "struggle" or "battle" with cancer. Cancer is a journey, and it's about living well, being kind and about loving more than you ever thought possible.

SOMEHOW THAT WINTER VANESSA managed to take Drivers Education and got her driver's license. I attempted to win her confidence by allowing her to drive me to the grocery store. Her capable hands gripped the steering wheel. I pressed myself into the passenger seat and clutched the armrest, my shoulders riding up.

"You aren't very relaxed," she observed. When the errand was completed and she pulled our car into the driveway I was thankful, and my mind burst into quiet relief. Feathers from a crow were scattered on the front lawn. Recently my friend Tim had told me that he needed more crow feathers to finish making new pow wow dance regalia. I went into the house to call Tim, then came back out and sat down on the front porch steps. The sun glowed gold and then deep red. I watched the sky for a long time. The air smelled of woodsmoke. Each breath I took smelled rich like the ground after a rainstorm. I watched the bats come out; they dipped and dived through the now dusky sky. It was quiet except for the crickets.

IN FEBRUARY OF 1999 Jay was three months past diagnosis and he continued to feel reasonably well. He held life in his two hands and was squeezing out its sweetest juices.

On good days he made himself a cup of cocoa, poured cold cereal into a bowl, and sat at the white tile breakfast bar, eating, and reading. The best days were when he didn't vomit. I kept the garbage disposal side of the sink empty, just in case. Brain tumors aren't like the flu. There wasn't any nausea, no warning, just a sudden wave. Even when he did throw up, he possessed complete good will and wholehearted forgiveness. He cleaned himself up, and a few minutes later he would go back to his meal. He didn't complain about having a brain tumor, he moved forward with his life. As ill as he was, he gave the impression he'd outlive all of us. But suddenly in March his voice grew raspy.

"It's really weird," Jay, said, "I just completely ran out of breath." The next day Jay had difficulty swallowing, and it was beginning to be hard for him to talk. His chest rattled when he breathed.

Jay was admitted to the hospital. The doctor came to talk with us. In a semi-private hospital room we conversed in low private whispers, while Jay's roommate, a sixteen-year-old boy who was an appendectomy patient, thumbed through pages of a sports magazine, pretending disinterest, giving us the illusion of privacy.

The news wasn't good. An MRI showed that the tumor was three times as big, and Jay's body was beginning to shut down. I blinked in surprise. Jay knit his brow as he let the news sink in. Gary and I sat feeling helpless while he was placed on oxygen, and a feeding tube was inserted.

"I'm not afraid to die," Jay said, "I just don't want to do it. But if it turns out that I have to, then I want to die at home."

I made a quick phone call to Hospice and left a message for someone to call me back. Someone from Hospice came to talk with us, and then for SIX HOURS we waited for the hospital paperwork to be competed, allowing Jay to leave. By now he could barely speak, his words were slurred, yet he was completely alert and fully coherent. He wrote notes when he wanted to tell us something.

I watched Jay's face, studied the tiny dark mole on the top of his right ear, and memorized the way his black hair shined red in sunlight from the window. It was the only thing I knew to do. It was not hard to talk to Jay about cancer. But I wondered how long it would be before he couldn't hear me anymore. I thought about the day when his body began to wear out, about the day when he stopped living.

Before Jay was released from the hospital, a nurse came to remove his feeding tube. Jay frowned, and he wrote me a note that said, "After they take it out, how am I going to eat?" Gary blinked back tears. My mouth remained open as I searched for a reply. I took a deep breath of hospital air that smelled of old wax and disinfectant.

"As your body begins to slow down, you probably won't be feeling hungry," I offered. We faced each other, not two feet apart, yet in different universes. Jay stiffened, drew back from me, then he punched me in the arm, hard.

A second later he pulled me close to him and gave me a light kiss on the cheek.

"We can ask them to leave the tube in," I suggested, "Just in case you get hungry."

TWELVE HOURS LATER, JAY WAS settled in at home. The dog gave him a welcome home lick. A Hospice nurse arrived and taught me how to care for Jay. I learned to operate the oxygen tanks. There were so many dials and valves and coils and hoses that at first it seemed too complicated. Frosty air escaped the overflow valve. Although I corrected the problem almost immediately, Jay's dark intelligent eyes regarded me with raw suspicion.

Usually it was Jay who taught *me* how to make things work. He programmed the VCR, he installed computer programs, and on driving trips he read the map and gave *me* directions. He was patient, he always took his time making sure things were exactly right. Suddenly time had been transformed from a resource into an unseen opponent.

We used the swabs Hospice provides with cool water and a bit of mint so Jay's mouth would feel fresh and clean. He relaxed when he realized the Hospice nurse wouldn't be poking him with needles as so many others had already done in the hospital. Jay had grown to hate the hospital; he was able to live so much more at home. At home everything was peaceful and familiar. We placed a hospital bed in the living room, and the cord on his oxygen was long enough so that he could move about and relax on the couch, allowing him to hear everything going on in the kitchen. Through the wall of windows stretching across the living room we watched the sky fall dark and fill with stars. Gary, Vanessa and I curled up with Jay on the couch; all of us cuddled together in that tight space. I watched Jay's face, and through the window I watched for shooting stars.

"Do you want me to sleep out here with you tonight?" I asked, thinking that amid all the oxygen tubes, the strange surrounding of the hospital bed in our living room, Jay would feel lonely and scared. His eyes lit up and he squeezed my hand. Dressed in sweats, I settled myself at his side. In the morning he felt well enough so that he was concerned about an order he'd placed through a catalog, and he wanted me to call and see if it had shipped out.

Although he had very low energy and napped off and on all day, when he was awake he was fully alert. He could no longer talk at all, and communicated by writing notes to us yet his jet black eyes spoke volumes.

At four o'clock Vanessa came home from school. Her friend Ray came over. Jay and Ray played a game of checkers, and Jay won the game. They watched television for a while, and then Jay said he had a headache. Morphine needed to be administered every six to eight hours for pain, yet all day Jay had remained pain-free so I hadn't given him any. I put on my glasses and carefully measured out one tiny drop. I practiced twice, to make sure I had the right amount and each time I let the liquid drip back into the bottle from the eyedropper. I gave Jay the tiny drop of morphine and helped him into bed and he fell asleep with the dog curled near the foot of the bed.

Vanessa left to go to a school choir rehearsal, and Gary and I sat near Jay's bed talking softly. A few minutes later I leaned over to check on Jay. I put my hand on his arm and my stomach froze tight; I could feel him slipping away.

"Squeeze my finger if you can hear me," I pleaded. Jay gave my finger a light squeeze; so weightless I could barely feel it. He slept in a classic fetal position, knees beneath his chest, occupying as small a space as possible. A few minutes later I spoke to Jay again, this time no response. Fear unraveled inside me. Gently I grabbed his wrist with my thumb and forefinger and counted a pulse.

At first I thought I must have given Jay too much morphine. Gary called Hospice, and the nurse insisted that I hadn't. It was an irrational feeling of me thinking of things I could have done differently which might have resulted in Jay being fully alert again.

Hospice offered to send someone over, but we preferred support by telephone.

Gary tried to telephone Vanessa to tell her to come home right away, but he was unable to reach her. And we didn't have a current phone number for Kyeong Sook. We didn't know where she lived. We had no way of contacting her.

All evening we sat at Jay's bedside. At eight o'clock his breathing stopped, and at that moment Vanessa walked in the door.

"I had feeling that I needed to come home," she said. "So I left right in the middle of choir rehearsal."

"Jay's dying," Gary called out. "Hurry."

Vanessa dropped her coat in the hall; she put her hand on Jay's chest and spoke to her brother. His eyebrows arched, but he didn't respond in any other way, yet we felt positive he could hear her. She folded herself onto the bed with him.

A few minutes later Gary and I climbed onto the bed too. Jay lay in the center among the three of us, small, quiet, immobile, with his dog at his side. Soon after he fell into a coma, yet we felt positive he could still hear us.

All night Jay's breathing stopped and then started again.

"Maybe we need to tell him that's it's okay to die," Vanessa offered. "Jay, I love you," she said. "Don't worry, I'll do your chores and help Mom. Time is different in heaven; we'll be there with you before you know it," she cooed. Gary and I sat with our arms around each other and tears pouring down our cheeks.

I kissed Jay on his forehead. "It's okay," I whispered. "Don't wait for anything, it's time for you to go."

We huddled around Jay and wished him a good journey as he crossed over to the other side. At that moment he smiled the sweetest smile, and a peaceful feeling as wide as the sky settled over us. Something warm and cozy fell across my heart. And then he was gone.

Rain began to fall, pounding the roof. As quick as it had arrived the cozy heaven feeling left. Gary, Vanessa and I agreed; it was as though a million years had passed. As though we had traveled with Jay to the faraway place beyond this life. We didn't wonder, we *knew* we had gone all the way to the point of entry with him. We didn't see the light; we felt it surround us. It pulled us, drew us in. For the briefest moment I wanted Jay to go. It felt right, like the most natural thing in the world. In that moment I was certain he was headed home.

Jay had only been gone for a few minutes, and we were plunged back to earth into a stark awareness that no longer held a living breathing Jay Trevor. Jay's body lay still and small, and we sat with his body in the hush just before dawn when darkness gives way to light. The peaceful smile on his face was preserved like a monument. I sat stroking his hands, tracing the creases in his palm, looking at each finger so gingerly separated with each syndactyly release surgery.

As I held his hand I thought about my great-great grandma who had given birth to eleven babies. The first died at four months, the second at age eight. It went on like that for years, grandma giving birth and grandpa making baby boards, digging holes and lowering those dead babies into the ground. It was a time of measles and small pox epidemic. My mind glimpsed my great-great grandma and I felt a distant memory pulling me back. I could hear her wailing like wind coming up, crying, swaying. I thought about how her cries probably drifted into the cabins of nearby white settlers, and I wondered if they knew the high, shrill sounds pressing against the night were from an Indian mother mourning her dead child.

DECISIONS ABOUT THE REMOVAL of Jay's body had to be made. Although I knew I had to, I couldn't bear to call the funeral home and have them come take him away. Gary made the phone call. Another miracle surfaced: the funeral director, though we did not know him personally, said that his church prayer line had been praying for Jay all night. He agreed to let us bring Jay's body to the mortuary ourselves. We wrapped him in the blue flannel sheets from his bed patterned with tiny snowmen. Vanessa drove because she wanted to drive. Gary was in no shape, and I didn't want to. I sat in the passenger seat, and Gary sat in the back with Jay's body wrapped in a small bundle on his lap.

We were lucky to be granted that one small grace, to take Jay's body to the funeral home ourselves. I felt the boundary of time collapse around me as if it had been one very long day since greeting one-year-old baby Jay at the airport in 1984 when he arrived from Korea. In the blink of an eye fourteen years had passed, allowing me the privilege of being his mother, and now night was setting in, closing Jay's life in a full circle.

All that day a long, steady stream of people came to our house. I had wanted to be still and quiet, to keep that peaceful feeling we all felt as Jay was leaving, inside me for as long as possible. But I couldn't because friends and family came to comfort us. I have no idea who was here; I wish I could remember who came.

## ⇒ THE WINTER JAY DIED, 1999 ⇐

The next day the telephone rang and Kyeong Sook sobbed on the other end of the line. "What happened?" she said, "It's Jay, isn't it?"

The mother of a high school friend had figured out how to contact her, explaining she needed to call home right away. The team of mothers I had long waited for to help me raise Kyeong Sook had finally arrived. Hours later Kyeong Sook walked through the front door. Surprisingly, it was a comfortable reunion, made relaxed by the fact that the house was so filled with all of our family and friends, and it was awful because Jay was dead. I hadn't seen Kyeong Sook in three years, and Jay had died less than twenty-four hours earlier.

I didn't want to have to behave in a normal manner and make attempts at conversation. I wanted to wail, to rock back and forth moaning and sobbing. There is a Paiute mourning ritual known as the Cry Dance, wherein the dancers and singers, clutching strips of clothing that belonged to the person who has died support the bereft as she fills the silence for a few minutes with her "cry"—the sound of human grief. I wished that a Cry Dance could be held for me because acting as if I had the ability to hold it all together was more than I could bear.

I got through those first days minutes at a time. My chest ached so much there were moments when I thought I might die from heartbreak. We were all doing the best we could. The world had been knocked out from under us and we were freefalling. Vanessa and Kyeong Sook had always lived a world apart. The roots of their uneasiness with each other stretched far back to the first day they met and lodged deep. They were just different from each other in ways that were extremely trivial and wildly profound. Over the years too many unresolved issues had piled up between them.

I longed to be one of those mothers who could be with both of my daughters at the same moment and have us feel relaxed with each other, instead of them feeling obligated to do it for my sake. It was my cross to bear. After all it had been my idea to make Vanessa and Kyeong Sook sisters, my idea and Gary's, and neither of us consulted them. We placed them together and turned both of their lives topsy-turvy. I had tried to keep my relationship with them as equal as possible; of course it didn't work, why would it? It's not a sane way to parent. By the time they were both teenagers, when I realized that there was too much friction for me to relax with both of them together at the same time, I began to cultivate separate, independent associations with each of them, and I kept my disappointment to myself. To an outside observer, an average sister relationship may have seemed intact. They got along well enough to be together all that week; both were all hospitality, generosity and warmth. But I knew that they had little interest in each other. Jay was the glue that held them together, and without Jay around any intimacy they felt with each other seemed to have ended. It ended immediately. Just like that.

TERRA TREVOR

THE RAIN CONTINUED ALL WEEK, and the roof began to leak in multiple places. The largest drip fell exactly above where Jay's hospital bed had sat in the living room. If he were still in that bed rain would have dripped on his pillow.

As we sat in the living room watching television, I felt a tap on the top of my head. I turned around to look and there wasn't anyone behind me. I wasn't in the mood to be teased and had a feeling of someone sneaking up on me. I kept whipping my head around to catch Gary or Vanessa in the act, yet they were both engrossed in the show and hadn't moved off the couch. I had the oddest feeling of someone else being in the room with us.

"What's the matter?" Gary asked.

"Someone just tapped me on the head." I admitted.

"We're watching Jay's favorite show," Vanessa announced. "It must have been him." She was joking of course.

A few minutes later I felt anther tap on my head. "Hey," I said. "It happened again."

When we left the house to go somewhere, after we got back home, we felt an odd sensation, as if Jay had gone with us. But obviously, he hadn't.

Condolence cards fanned out on the table. On the bookshelf there was a photograph of me, taken by Jay, in which I'm standing in the ocean. When I looked at this picture, I remembered the grin on Jay's face and the wave that washed over me seconds after the snapshot was taken.

I sat staring beyond the window, watching the wind turn wild and bend the branches of the oak trees. Above my head hung the thousand paper cranes. The paper birds glittered in the stream of sun, and the wind whipping through the slightly opened living room window made the birds rustle and sway.

Memorial service planning began. Reverend Lee the pastor of our Korean church had retired five years earlier, and it had been a while since I last spoke with him. We picked up right where we left off, as if no amount of time had passed. His white hair shone in the morning sun, and wild flowers bloomed in the field behind us as we made our plans.

Vanessa and Reverend Lee gave a eulogy at Jay's memorial service. Nearly all of those from our Korean church were present. Nearly everyone we knew from all aspects of our lives was present. A friend sang Amazing Grace in Korean, and elders said prayers in the Korean language. If religion and ceremonies are the heart of a culture, then language is the lifeblood. A calm washed over me I hadn't felt in days. More than three hundred people came to pay their respects, and everyone couldn't fit inside the chapel, so the guests spilled outside into the courtyard. Scanning the crowd, I saw the faces of everybody I knew, hundreds of familiar faces, even those who had to drive for miles. We laughed and cried together, and one by one, we hugged each of them, Jay's friends, their parents, his teachers, our friends, our neighbors, Vanessa and Kyeong Sook's friends, and their parents. Everyone we knew came to support us. Another friend captured all those hugs and tears on film.

After the memorial service a large group of family and friends came to our home, where more friends were already gathered preparing food. Ahryun telephoned from Sweden so that she could be a part of it all. The sun came out, and we filled the yard with people laughing and weeping. A basketball game was in process, and someone pulled out the checkerboard. It was the kind of gathering Jay liked best; he would have enjoyed the day, and who knows, maybe he did.

A few days later we went out on the Star Dust, the boat Jay always fished from, and scattered his ashes in the ocean, in the spot where he once caught a thirty-eight-pound halibut.

# ⇒ SPRING, 1999 ⇐

I awoke at 3:00 AM. The night air was thick with skunk, clear and cool. I was living at survival level. My life, as I'd known it up to then, was over. Before I had a son to raise, and now I didn't. Kyeong Sook, along with the last guests, had packed her belongings and had gone home. We were no longer estranged, yet we hadn't really connected either.

Everyone kept warning me not to isolate. Yet nearly all of my friends had children adopted from Korea. Should I continue to attend adoptive family gatherings? After fourteen years of parenting children adopted from Korea, and carving out friendships with other adoptive families, being around them was a big reminder that my days of being an adoptive parent were over. I had been invited to speak at the first KAAN National Conference on Korean Adoptions (Korean American Adoptee Adoptive Family Network). A dynamic I once viewed as a climb towards success now only reminded me of what I'd lost.

I got out of bed and sat before the window looking out into the dark shapes of trees. The moon, in a corner of the sky, was full and wide, and my thoughts, heavy saddlebags. I pulled a coat over my nightgown and walked out into the damp air, and squeezed out the tears. A spider web stretched across the path. I paused sleepily, listening to the crickets. All of a sudden it occurred to me that Jay's birth family had no way of knowing he was dead. What if they should decide to come forward and try to locate him?

In the morning I contacted a friend in Korea and faxed her a copy of the eulogy Reverend Lee gave at Jay's memorial service written in Hangul. Then I gave her the address and asked her to write a letter and send it to Sun Rak Won. The eulogy Reverend Lee wrote, saying he thought of Jay as his own grandchild, gave a personal glimpse into our lives.

In less than a week I received an e-mail response letting me know my correspondence had been placed in Jay's file at Sun Rak Won.

Next I sat down and wrote to Holt in Korea and sent them a copy of Reverend Lee's eulogy. Two weeks later I received a letter from Holt.

Dear Mr. & Mrs. Trevor,

First of all, we don't know what to say. We are very sorry to hear news like this. This, is by far, the most difficult letter I've read while working as a social worker for Holt. We do remember Jay's visit to Korea last summer. To our memories he seemed to enjoy life thoroughly and was very happy. After receiving your letter we went back to our files and looked at photos of Jay. The smile on his face in the photos is the way we remember him. He had a very distinguished smile that nobody would be able to forget. At least we never will here at Holt in Korea.

Sincerely yours,

The letter was signed by the Supervisor of Post Placement Services and the Director of Overseas Adoption. I remembered meeting all three of them at Holt in Seoul. Probably, since Jay and I had been invited to Holt as representatives of the Friends of Korea Family Exchange Program, our visit entailed more formality than usual. Our meeting was also more intimate than the average adoptee visit. I have no doubt the intimacy was due to Jay's own personality and his ability to let others know their generosity was appreciated.

I had done all that I could for Jay. I felt a lump in my throat knowing one day his birthmother might learn of his death, and then, at that moment, her grieving for him would begin with piercing raw aching, the kind of pain and sorrow that now surrounded me. Then the gap opened for me and I saw fully, grasped the whole understanding and felt the grief journey that began for her the moment Jay was born. His fingers misshapen, growing tightly fused together on both of his hands. I imagined how she must have prayed for a miracle in the four or so months that she kept him. Of the despair holding her hostage the afternoon she left him at Sun Rak Won, and the searing pain she must have felt waking up in the morning without him.


THE WEEKS AFTER JAY'S DEATH rolled by faster than I wanted them to, taking me further away from Jay. My heart folded over like a candle melting in on itself each time new acquaintances asked me the question, "How many children do you have?"

What felt most isolating, Gary, Vanessa and I agreed, was without Jay in our family circle we didn't have anything or anyone to identify us as Asian. New people in our lives would never guess that in the center of our hearts we felt connected to Korean ethnicity.

After Jay died things just kept growing more difficult. Next our dog Sadie, the rock of our family, our cherished Newfoundland now grown old, began having difficulty breathing. Her chest rattled and she gasped for air. We took her to the vet, he checked her over and then told us what we already knew. Instead we went home to think it over.

Vanessa gave Sadie a spoonful of vanilla ice cream. Sadie slurped at it with puppy-like zest. We petted and cuddled her. My memory recalls Jay being with us that day, only he couldn't have been.

Later in the afternoon when Sadie was getting worse, we knew it was time to let her go. The vet arranged for us to have a room to ourselves for as long as we needed. I knelt down by Sadie and gently stroked her. Gary, Vanessa and I petted her as the overdose of anesthesia made its swift deadly way. Outside the vets' office we three stood weeping.

This time grief and sorrow lodged in Vanessa's jaw. The dentist had her wear a mouth splint day and night. For weeks she lived on blender drinks and smoothies. She was irritable and hair-triggered. The sound of her unhappiness ranged from yelling to extended crying. Sunlight glittered in from the window. I watched her greet the morning by banging the blender on the counter as she prepared her breakfast.

"Hey," I said, using my most soothing tone of voice.

"I've lost so much weight," she snapped. "None of my jeans fit me."

I put my hand on the small of her back; she was thin as a chopstick, her hip bones looked sharp enough to push through the soft folds of her jeans. That's when I wanted to burst into tears because I knew I couldn't buy her a smaller size pair, not this month anyway.

The stream of sun from the window grew diffuse and the early morning warmth was gone. The room felt cold. I made myself a cup of coffee and began my day. I confronted the refrigerator. We were low on milk, but there were plenty of eggs. I thought about frying up a couple and then changed my mind; better save the eggs to make an omelet for dinner.

Usually Vanessa bought many of her own clothes from money she earned babysitting. But recently I'd insisted she cut back on her work hours. The flu hit her hard twice since Jay died, and she needed extra rest. Still lack of money seemed a silly reason not to buy her a new pair of jeans. When Jay was terminally ill from cancer, I bought him a new pair of sweat pants, knowing he'd only need them for a short time.

I was tired of thinking about money, but my stomach clinched around the words anyway. At least I was working again, yet business was slow for Gary now, and we were back to making ends meet. Living on a tight budget didn't usually bother me, though there had been more expenses than usual lately, a new roof on the house and car repair expenses. I didn't care about luxury, just as long as I could pay the utility bills, buy groceries and still have enough money left over to buy new pants for my kids when they shrank to a smaller size.

I finished my coffee and blinked back tears. Poor Vanessa not only lost her brother to death, she also lost her parents to grief. Though I wished I had the power to uplift Vanessa, I didn't. I was barely coping. Gary couldn't do it either; he clung with all his might to hang on to his own sanity. We tried, but we didn't have much within us to help each other. I imagined us each in a tiny rowboat, drifting alone, in a stormy sea. Now I am able to see that in our first year of bereavement we were right where we were supposed to be, but I didn't know it at the time.

Luckily I never felt like denying myself pleasure, not even in the first few weeks or months. I still tried to watch movies and read books and walk on the beach. In a grief support group I met a mother who said she didn't want to laugh or eat delicious food or go anywhere out of respect for her dead child. That mother also said her anger was so raging she couldn't even stand to see the flowers blooming in her yard. She said, "How dare those flowers blare open to face the sun." She wanted to put weed killer on them so they would look as bad as she was feeling. I'd discovered that type of reaction was fairly common, and I was grateful my grief didn't lead me down that path.

Fortunately, very fortunately, we had a wide network of family and friends to keep us shored up. We managed as well as it is possible to manage so soon after the death of a son and brother. Gary and I went to work, we remembered to pay the utility bills, and checked the oil level in the car. Vanessa kept her grades up, and I helped her fill out college applications. She had planned to go away to school, yet after Jay died she wanted to give the idea up and attend a college close to home. Even though I would have liked to keep Vanessa near me, in my heart of hearts I knew it was best to help her stick with her original plan and to follow her dreams.

My plans for parenthood sat like scenery on an empty stage. I wasn't ready to have an empty nest, yet I didn't want Vanessa to feel she had to stay home because of me. She needed the experience of living on a college campus full-time, and I needed to come up with a new life for myself. But how could I choose my destiny when I couldn't even buy a new sweater without exchanging it twice before deciding on a color and the right fit. I was starting my life over from scratch, and I was terrified of making decisions, even little ones.

I didn't think I would ever care about anything ever again. My mind felt glued shut, and my heart was beginning to feel like it was laminated, sealed in plastic to keep out further pain. Then I had a soul-bleaching moment when I understood that I didn't want to stay closed up and hollow feeling forever. There had to be a way to allow myself the space and time to grieve deep and fully, and feel every ounce of the pain, and yet continue to walk forward. Jay, a pole star in my life had passed. I would never get over it. Nor would I ever be the same. I would not give up or give in to society's mistaken notion of getting over grief fast in order to get on with my life. I would find a way to learn to live with grief and not allow it to hold me back.

The answer came when I remembered a family vacation to the state of Washington. We went to Mt. St. Helens and Jay and I stared at the way she looked years after her summit was removed by a volcanic eruption. That day I stood watching the slate blue dusk blend into ragged peaks and lava domes. A friend once had a cabin perched on a bluff overlooking the lake, surrounded by gigantic pines. I pulled up the hood of my sweatshirt, my face strained into the wind. Fireweed and purple-red flowers dotted the level earthen floor in a place where a forest and the cabin once stood. We walked, circling the crater, and saw wild violets blooming.

The mountain had been scattered and sundered into bits, and she survived. I swallowed a clotty grief deep inside my throat. A grief so wide it gave me laryngitis. Bold and enthusiastic thoughts of Jay filled me. I was breathing proof he was once more than a photograph.

I shuffled out into the empty field of my mind to find enough words to make it through another winter of writing. Nothing quits. My life had changed into something I didn't want, and I began gathering the pieces that were left of me, and coaxing them into growth. I was starting out again, but like the mountain, I'd lost all of my big trees.

The horizon was still mine. I felt myself part of the mountain with hills catching the sunset through a furious wind, dust devils kicking up dirt. All my senses became alive, out on the edge. I imagined fireweed blooming on the burned over land in my heart, beginning purple petals.

## ⊰ SPRING, 2000 ⊱

We had completed a long year of firsts: My first Mother's Day without Jay, and Gary's first Father's Day. We moved through Jay's sixteenth birthday without him, followed two weeks later by the shared day Jay and Lynne arrived from Korea; the day Jay became our treasured son, a grandson and a brother.

I knew some adoptive parents referred to their child's arrival as "Gotcha Day."

It was an unfortunate term. Receiving a child is a sacred occasion. "Gotcha" took away from a birthmother's loss, and only focused on an adoptive parent's gain. In the Lakota language the word for child means, "stands sacred." The English language does not carry words powerful enough to convey. I've always felt it was important to hold our children's arrival day in awe and celebrate without feeling a need to name it anything other than what it represented: The day Jay arrived from Korea.

Even though rituals were important to me, we had no idea how to observe the first anniversary of Jay's death; the day his soul returned from where it came. We spent every day remembering Jay, so I didn't see how it made sense to designate the actual date of his death for this purpose. Wasn't it better to celebrate his fifteen years on earth, every day of our lives?

My mind was centering on these thoughts the afternoon Vanessa began begging me to buy her a pair of red satin pants. Gary was with us, and we were at a bargain outlet mall.

"But these pants are marked way down," Vanessa pleaded.

"Where on earth would you wear them?" I queried. "It would make sense if you wanted to get them for a special occasion, but where would you go in them?"

"I'm alive Mom," Vanessa said. "I could wear them whenever I was in the mood to wear them. If I woke up and felt like putting on these wonderful red pants and wearing them to school, then I could do it because I'm alive!"

Gary and I looked at each other. We both had tears in our eyes. We looked at Vanessa. She had tears in her eyes too. Gary then tossed the red pants in our shopping cart, and we three stood in the middle of the store crying until we started laughing.

Thus a tradition began. In our family March 11<sup>th</sup> has become the day each year when we light a candle and renew our vows to be kind and gentle with ourselves, to treat ourselves and each other well, to honor each other because we are still alive. We're still here, living and loving, and that's what life is all about.


FOR MY BIRTHDAY THAT YEAR in April of 2000, Gary gave me a gift certificate to get a massage. I peeled down to my underwear, stretched out on the massage table and pulled the white flannel sheet up around my armpits. I wiggled my bare toes. The massage therapist pressed her hands into the small of my back. I felt my muscles relax. I have spent the equivalent of years of my life wishing for massages. If I had a weekly massage, I believed maybe my torso would grow supple, my legs long and nimble. This was as good as it got. I'd hit pay dirt. I tried to hush my thoughts, forced myself not to think about any worries. Her fingers moved up and down my leg. I let my middle-aged brain float without any barriers. Ravens flew through my mind, and a soothing feeling spread over me like sun-warmed rainwater floating down my neck and shoulders and glided over me like feather-down wings.

Then suddenly a cat hopped on top of me and was extremely affectionate; he kneaded the bed sheet on my lower back, purred, his whole body rumbled with cat pleasure.

Then the cat leaped off of me. I let out a giggle and then my tense body relaxed even more. My head relaxed, my neck and down to my chest and into the lines and curves of my abdomen. Outside the streetlights came on. From somewhere in the distance a radio played a Mexican polka. I felt all the parts of my body as if I'd never before knew they were all there at the same time. The air grew blue dark, and a passing car reflected the corner streetlight outside. I lay mindless and eternal, wondering how to gain my senses enough to drive home.

# ⁊ SUMMER, 2000 ⁊

Vanessa graduated from high school in June, and two weeks later she began a full-time summer job as a camp counselor.

Jay had only been dead for a little over a year, and already well-meaning friends had begun to treat us as if our grief warranty had expired. Some of our friends and co-workers hinted that it had been long enough, and that we should be getting on with our lives. It had become painfully clear "getting on with our lives" to some people meant avoiding Jay's name in conversations. This irked me. A person could sell their medical practice and retire, and forever after they would be referred to as doctor. Yet after fourteen years of being mother to Jay there were some who viewed motherhood spent on a child who had died as an era that should no longer be acknowledged. If only those people understood moving on didn't mean erasing our past.

We *were* getting on with our lives. On weekends Gary still fished with his fishing buddies, and he'd begun to make an even wider circle of fishing friends within the Asian community. Vanessa maintained her regular activities, yet she was bored with what now felt like mindless entertainment. She began to gravitate towards volunteer work, searching for a place where she could make a difference in the lives of others.

I was faced with the task of redefining myself. While I identified as a writer, the job that held the most meaning to me was being a mother. At the end of the summer Vanessa would leave for college. Jay's death meant that I was suddenly plunged into a role for which there was no name—a mother whose child has died.

I felt myself growing stronger and weaker. The stronger I became the more willing I was to allow myself to explore the depth of my sorrow. In my private life and with a few of my closest friends I didn't try to cover up my searing pain. I felt strong enough to let my guard down, exposing how weak I really felt, knowing I wouldn't be swallowed up by darkness. It was necessary to dig deep and search my feelings, and these periods were followed by fallow times where I let myself absorb what was.

Yet it was also clear life demanded me to cultivate a professional, almost clinical, side of myself that I could take out into the world, looking like I had it fairly together. For some reason there is the notion that one year is an acceptable timetable for grieving. Then we are expected to bounce back. Everyone expected us to remain pretty much the same as we were and to just bounce back with a limp. Yet grieving that lasted longer than a year was viewed as being stuck, abnormal, and not able to move forward.

After the first year my friends worried about me most when my heart still broke easily into pieces or when my fallow times kept me quieter than usual.

Yet the feeling of needing to seem like I was beginning to get it together scared me most. Acting stronger than I really was meant I might work too many long hours without coming up for air, or not cry at the sad part of movies when everyone else was crying.

Then I began to notice fear in the eyes of my friends. What every mother feared most had happened to me; I represented their worst nightmare. No doubt some could not bear to think about how awful it would be to bury their own child along with all of their hopes and dreams. I could tell that seeing me shattered, clawing my way back to center, was a horror beyond their worst terror imaginable.

In an effort to ease their discomfort and my own, I began to push myself too fast and behave as I thought I should: As if I had my wrenching grief under control, and was beginning to get my life in sync.

THAT SUMMER I WAS INVITED to travel to Korea to spend two weeks assisting with the Friend's of Korea Family Exchange Program. When I opened a suitcase to begin packing I found my gray fleece sweatshirt inside. Jay wore it last. Near the end he lost so much weight his own jacket was too big and he practically lived in my fleece. Then I saw a great big, blob of modeling glue on the outside of the left pocket, about the size of a quarter, dried rock hard. My first thought was "Jay, you've ruined my fleece."

For a split second it was as if he wasn't dead, and I could walk into his room and give him a hard time, and everything would be normal again.

I couldn't bear the thought of going to Korea without Jay. But I also couldn't bear the thought of not going to Korea. I have no idea how I found the courage and strength. Early grief is exhausting. Everything took too much effort. It's a good thing I didn't need a new passport.

Two close friends, Terri and Gail and their daughters, were also traveling to Korea with Friends of Korea. Terri is like a sister, and Gail is like a cousin to me. Our kids grew up together, and they were like cousins. More than eighteen years together made us family to each other.

Without Jay, I boarded the plane with Terri and Gail and their daughters, and we headed for Korea.

I planted my feet on Korean pavement. Summer sweltering air scented with sesame blasted me in the face. The sun baked into my skin. All around me horns honked, and people swarmed the sidewalks. My heart soared. I squinted at the sky.

"I'm here. I'm here." I kept thinking. What I was feeling was almost a prayer. I didn't expect to feel happy; the feeling snuck up on me. Then I knew if I could go to Seoul without Jay and still feel ripples of happiness, then I would be able to do anything.

Terri and Gail, along with eight other American families, would spend the first week with their Korean host family. My job was to help my friend Christy Winston, founder and program president, trouble shoot and problem solve. Then in the second week, when all of the American families would be together in Seoul, my job was to help keep things running smooth as possible while Chris attended the endless meetings and required social events that surfaced unexpectedly.

The first time I had traveled to Korea with Kyeong Sook and Vanessa we stayed at an orphanage. It was a poor orphanage, and we had barely enough to eat. My second time in Korea with Jay we stayed with an upper middle class family for a week and enjoyed many privileges. Next Jay and I stayed in a cheaper priced hotel in Seoul and learned about scrappy city life.

But on my third trip to Korea I found myself staying at the home of wealthy friends, a twenty-minute subway ride from the city. We were in a rural feeling neighborhood with upscale restaurants and grocery stores nearby. After dinner we walked tree-lined paths with the sound of thousands of cicadas and the moon rising early, reflecting slivery light. I've never been one who required expensive luxurious accommodations. Though if ever there was a time in my life for me to experience what being rich felt like, that was when I needed it most. My emotions were needy while my body was pampered with the best of comforts.

I don't remember all of the events of those two weeks in Korea in chronological order. In my mind a juxtaposition of vivid scenes, when prompted, pop up and open to me like windows on a computer.

There was the meeting in Seoul I was invited to attend. We dressed in our business best, and after the long, formal meeting adjourned, the chairman of the Visit Korea Commission invited us to lunch. We dined at Korea House Restaurant in one of the traditional rooms where we sat on the floor at a large round table. It was something I had always wanted to do. After we finished eating many bowls of the best Korean foods, while I was sipping barley tea, the chairman of the Visit Korea Commission asked, "How many children do you have?"

His question slid out effortlessly. As if it were the most natural question in the world to ask.

I froze, with my teacup in my hand. I opened my mouth but could not form the words. He straightened his back and rolled his shoulders just slightly while waiting for me to answer.

"Two." I replied. "I've got two daughters."

My friend Christy looked at me with her mouth open, the expression on her face was the same as if she had just seen a ghost. My friend Eyoungsoo stared at me too, with his mouth open. Then Eyoungsoo said, "Only two? You only have two children?"

I wanted to take my statement back and share my story but I couldn't. It was the worst moment in my life. It felt like Jay died again, and this time I killed him.

Later I told my friends it was just too hard. If I told about Jay I knew I would cry. It was funny because even at the time I knew this was one of those social business situations where it would be all right. These people would understand, and in the end it would draw us closer.

It was the moment that would define me. It ravaged me and took me down, like chemo attacking a cancer. Then I rose up, healed.

I never did it again. I had tried out a new identity of meeting the world as the mother of two daughters, and not mentioning my son who had died. The image of leaving out Jay left a horrible hole in my heart. It left me a stranger, I didn't know myself. If I didn't claim Jay then I might as well not claim anything or anybody in my past. One thing remained certain: For the rest of my life I knew my answer would always be, "I had three children, and one died."

That afternoon, after the business luncheon ended, our friend Eyoungsoo took us on a surprise excursion. Chris and I giggled in the back seat like teenage girls. We had no idea where we were headed, only that we were leaving the city. Two hours later our car stopped. Trees lined the road. We walked down a long pathway that led to a house in a wooded area alongside the Han-gang river. Other friends greeted us at the door. Everyone wore shorts with casual shirts and bare feet. Chris and I were wearing heels and nylons, skirts and business suit jackets.

We were led to a large deck along side the river and the idea was to spend the day swimming or wading, or paddling the rowboat if we wanted. But in our business suits?

The owner of the house offered to let us borrow shorts. Only this was a man's vacation home, and there wasn't any women's clothing. I was loaned a set of men's matching Hawaiian print shorts and shirt, because it was the only thing small enough to fit me. Chris ended up wearing gym shorts and a T-shirt.

In the middle of that glorious afternoon we were told to go select a pair of sandals from the pile near the door, because we were going to take the boat and cross the river to go to the lodge for a drink.

We sorted through the stack, but the pairs of rubber thongs were twice as big as our feet.

The boat docked and we tried not to laugh too much as we walked into the fancy lodge overlooking the river, wearing our funny clothes, with our great big rubber sandals flopping.

Lunch was served. I began munching hot chili peppers. All eyes focused on me. Then a man in our group began urging me to eat whole garlic cloves. He was amazed to see my delight.

"She eats like a Korean man," Someone said.

Thus my reputation was born. Later that evening at dinner all sorts of Korean foods I'd never eaten were placed before me. My new friends watched me eat. The more I ate the more food they heaped in front of me.

The next day I traveled by train to Masan with a friend, to keep her company while her daughter spent time with her birth parents. From the train window I began to spot burial mounds scattered along the countryside. Grass grew on older graves. Newer mounds were still covered with fresh earth. Some of the mounds were small and others much larger. Occasionally plastic tarps covered the mounds. As we passed through cities I saw funeral wreaths on the gates of houses. I saw funerals in progress. I kept my eyes peeled and began to notice people wearing white, which is the color for mourning in Korea. That was when I knew that if I were to die while I was in Korea, I would want my body to be left in Korea and be buried in a mound on the outskirts of town.

Although being with adoptive parents magnified the fact that, without Jay and Kyeong Sook, I was no longer doing any active adoptive parenting, it was the group of parents where I felt safest. When anyone outside of the adoption community made comments suggesting my grief, since Jay was adopted, might somehow be less than it would have been if he was my birth child, I felt further shattered. It also let me know mainstream attitudes towards adoption were still in the dark ages.

I was terribly jealous of my friends whose children were alive. It wasn't a sensible jealousy, and it made me feel guilty. Yet when was jealousy ever sensible? I never told any of my friends I was jealous because I knew in time I would get past it, and my friends might not. Even though it was uncomfortable, I wanted to be with other adoptive moms and their children because I wanted to live as close to normal as possible, instead of hiding out, protecting myself from pain and hurt.

In the early days of the trip, though, there was one night when I fell apart. I don't remember where we were. The date, however, I'm positive was August 5, 2000 because I wrote it down in my journal.

All of the American families with Friends of Korea were together. After a long day of train travel we stopped at a hotel. It was almost dinnertime, and everyone began making plans. Chris left for a dinner meeting, and I stayed in the hotel lobby overseeing the group. I listened in as the large group of parents and children decided whether they wanted to eat Korean or American food. Finally the group divided themselves into three groups. One group wanted to eat at an American style restaurant in the hotel, another wanted to go into town and scout around, and a third wanted to go down the block for a Korean meal. I made sure each group felt comfortable going off on their own and had directions to get back to the hotel. Then off they went.

I deliberately hung back alone. I stood by myself watching the groups of happy parents and children chatting and laughing together until they disappeared from sight.

All I knew was that I wanted to be alone. The sun was beginning to set and the sky was washed in yellow-orange light. I set off in the opposite direction from where my friends had gone. After a quarter of a mile the sidewalk turned towards the riverbed. I heard children's voices. From a distance I saw groups of Korean families gathered. Kids erupted with laughter. As I moved closer I could see they were driving little remote control cars along the concrete riverbed. It was the same kind of remote control cars Jay liked to play with. I perched myself at the edge of the riverbed and watched the families play together. There was a restaurant nearby, and from an outdoor speaker lilting Korean music played an instrumental tune. I watched the sunset, and then for at least half an hour I watched the families play and listened to the music. And then I began crying. I cried so hard everyone stared at me. I'm sure they noticed me when I first walked up, since I'm obviously not Asian, and I was a woman alone. But when I started crying everyone stopped and stared. I walked down the river away from the group and cried and cried until my head felt like it would burst. When I opened my blurry eyes, the stars were out, and I saw my life anew.

I look back at this night as the beginning of the new normal. My whole sense of who I was had burned. Inch-by-inch I was growing back. A new me was developing. Parts of me resembled the way I used to be, yet there were new aspects of myself now, and new ways I viewed the world that was shaped by my love for Jay and from learning to live without him.

I began to understand that I needed to cry and grieve the loss of my former self as much as I needed to grieve Jay's death.

I've heard people say that after the death of someone you can't live without, after you come through, it's like having a broken leg that never heals perfectly. You can still dance, but with a limp. That night I knew for certain I would not always dance with a limp. I knew it would take years, yet eventually my legs would grow stronger than before and carry me forward. My time with Jay made me better. It shaped me into a more loving, caring person with unshakeable faith. I knew things would probably get harder before I found my way though the maze of grief. But some day I would dance whole again, with a newfound rhythm.

With moonlight to guide me, I followed my way back to the families playing with remote control cars. There were only a few people now.

Suddenly I was hungry. I walked towards the hotel, and spotted a Korean restaurant. Inside I found a group from Friends of

Korea, and they asked me to join them. Within minutes I was eating and laughing, but with newfound gusto.

For the rest of my time in Korea I began to be able to look forward to things. In the past months I had never wanted to look forward because usually it didn't feel like there would be anything fun ahead. But now I understood that while nothing felt as fun as it did when Jay was alive, I could still find pleasant hours tucked into each day, and it was a beginning.

Looking forward meant when our travel companions voted to eat American food, Terri and I would take off together and go to a Korean restaurant and order big bowls of hot spicy *mandu* soup or *kimchi tchigae*. My barely-passing Korean language skills caused us to have some interesting combinations of food brought to us, since I couldn't understand what the waitress said to us. We nodded our heads yes and ate whatever they served us.

I saw preteen girls on the streets in Pusan in and around the fish market district. Girls too young to be out alone at night, wore that same look of capable confidence and vulnerability Kyeong Sook wore when she arrived from Korea. I began to grasp an understanding of the kind of life Kyeong Sook probably left behind. They say that the oldest child has the worst of it in most families, suffering from all the mistakes his or her parents don't have enough experience to avoid. It struck me that Kyeong Sook had two rookie mothers to contend with; the mom she had for the first ten years of her life in Korea, and then she had to start out all over again with me.

Near the end of the trip I realized I'd packed too much stuff, and I started leaving a trail behind me. After all the business ended I left my black heels behind. They were perfectly good new shoes and they were beginning to get ruined from being smashed into my suitcase. So I left them in the closet. Maybe one of the hotel maids might want them.

When I packed up my suitcase to travel to a new location, instead of sitting on my bag and squeezing the zipper shut, I chose something perfectly good to leave behind. Each time I left something behind it made me laugh. I joked to myself that I was "putting my past behind me," that awful expression some people used when they wanted to seek a future free of pain. I wished I could let those suffering souls in on the secret: When my memories didn't make me sad, they made me feel happy, grateful and lucky.

On my last night in Korea a bird landed on my windowsill and sang to me, not loud, but clear, high and true. Our room was on the third floor, high above the trees. It was a good omen.

## ⸢ FALL, 2OOO ⸣

On Labor Day weekend in September, two weeks before leaving for college, Vanessa brought home a puppy. She had just returned from working as a summer camp counselor at Camp Ronald McDonald where eleven puppies were born during the summer. The puppies were eight weeks old, and the camp staff knew they had to find homes for them.

"I'm not sure I'm ready for another dog," I groaned.

"You'll be lonely without me," Vanessa cooed.

I followed her outside with the pup. The day was bright and sunny with the faint colors of autumn emerging in the scrub oak. I looked at Vanessa and saw the totality of her, the first time I saw her face in the hospital delivery room, the first time I held her in my arms, her first sentence. I remembered Vanessa at age four, walking into her bedroom at the first light of dawn and finding her wearing only a black velvet beret and nylon fairy wings with loose elastic straps looped over her shoulders.

"I'm going to a party, she whispered, "Would you like to come?" Her barely slept in pajamas would be discovered later, when I searched the narrow space between the bed and the wall.

Vanessa was nineteen and about to leave home. While I was happy for her, the usually tiny cyst on my ankle had begun swelling to peach size, just like it had when we found out that Jay had the second brain tumor. In a wholly new way I was thrilled to see Vanessa for the first time in months take charge of what she wanted. Which at the moment meant she wanted me to have this dog. I watched her, tanned skin, rolling her too serious eyes, car keys in her hand. I could not gather back one moment of her childhood, only enjoy what came next. I felt my old self crawl out from under an imagined rock. It began to dawn on me that I was delighted. She was the perfect dog, mountain born, mixed breed, calm and going to be big.

"I'm going to call her Jenny," I announced. I cradled the puppy and nuzzled her soft neck. I felt her heart thumping, her breath quick and marvelous.

I settled in with Jenny the new puppy, and on a sunny mid-September day Vanessa left for college. She moved to a room on campus where she ate her meals in a communal dining hall in a dorm that never quieted down.

A few days later Vanessa called home telling me that a childhood friend was also attending the college. Lia and Vanessa had grown up together. They met through our Korean adoption support group, and were like cousins throughout much of their elementary school years, and then they lost touch in high school. Now they were reunited and struck up a new friendship. Vanessa was 400 miles from home, riding her bike to class and figuring out what the university seemed to be all about. I was able to peek into Vanessa's world when she emailed copies of her college essays to me.

Vanessa wrote, *Looking back on my life in the last year has really put into perspective how much growing up I have done. I am no longer the person I was in high school. Things such as paying bills, living with roommates, and being responsible for my schoolwork have caused me to become a much more responsible person. I no longer have the option of asking my parents for help; it's all up to me. Going away to college was the best decision I ever made. I have met so many people and have been exposed to so many diverse experiences that could never compare to my life before. I wouldn't trade them for anything.*

*I've been lucky enough to enroll in a Native American Studies class taught by a native Guatemalan immigrant who moved to the states because of the turmoil going on against the Mayan people. I took his class thinking that it would deal with American Indians and our history. Although the class did include those topics, it had a much greater focus on indigenous people such as the Mayan, Incas, and Aztecs. These are cultures that I never knew much about. Before taking this class I never considered those groups to be Native Americans. It never occurred to me that the term Native American refers to the indigenous people of all the Americas. As a result of this class I was able to get in contact with some prominent figures in the Native American studies department. I have hopes of becoming more involved with the program. Once a year they put on one of the best pow wows in the country.*

In another essay Vanessa wrote, *Over the summer I was able to work as a counselor at Camp Ronald McDonald for Good Times, a camp for cancer patients and their siblings. I worked with twelve- and thirteen-year-old girls, living with them and attending every activity with them. I also attended this camp as a child along with my sister, and with my brother who died from a brain tumor and cancer two years ago when he was fifteen. Being able to give back to an organization that gave me so much helps me deal with the loss of my brother. Camp is something I look forward to all year long. It is a place where I truly feel at home and as though everyone around me understands me to a degree that none of my friends at college can. Everyone at camp has gone through similar experiences that bond us together like nothing else.*

Usually Vanessa telephoned often, and in a relaxed talkative mood she began sharing details of her new life with me, a stream of consciousness that ran from what she'd done over the weekend and trailing the conversation into future plans she might expand on that in her mind were sound and logical. I began giving Vanessa the lowdown on how I felt about what she'd just told me.

We almost began a heated argument, and we would have except that she said, "Stop it, Mom. You have to be willing to just listen to my ideas without always giving me advice."

I took a deep breath, and all at once, realized that her problems were no longer my problems. That no matter how much I wanted to guide her towards success and protect her from ever having to experience any dangers or failures as she walked towards adulthood and independence, I couldn't.

"OK," I said, "I guess it's time for me to give you to yourself."

She giggled and replied, "Yes, you'd better, because my roommates parents refuse to do it, and they won't talk about everything the way I do; they just tell their parents what they think they want to hear." Then without missing a beat she continued telling me about her week.

"Last night my roommates and I went to a party in Berkeley."

"A party? You were at a party in Berkeley on a school night?" I gasped.

"Mom, stop it. Because, when you have too many opinions about my life you create a wall between us, and you've just put up another brick."

I forced myself to be quiet and listen, really listen to what she had to say.

"Yes, last night my room mates and I went to a party in Berkeley, and on the way home they were talking about how odd it felt to be the only ones at the party who were not Asian. Seriously, Mom, I never even noticed that everyone was Asian except us," she said.


MEANWHILE, KYEONG SOOK also had begun telephoning regularly. It was enormous for me to have her back in my life. At first it was odd when I realized we didn't have much to say to each other. We couldn't pick up the conversation where we left off, because we had never figured out how to communicate with each other. I would cautiously ask questions. Then there were those long awkward silences, and after that we both would start talking at the same time. Our entire relationship had been based in a period of time when she was a sad and miserable child. Our past was like broken bones that had not yet healed. I kept my guard up and didn't talk about anything emotional, because then roles we had played in the past could reemerge. I was trying to figure out how to let her know that I wanted to live with what was and stop struggling.

Over a matter of months we finally managed to build a good rapport by keeping to very light topics such as movies we'd seen and had both liked, or we talked about books and food. But the conversation never seemed to swing back around to anything personal because she shared very few details of her inner life. Yet she gave me her telephone number and encouraged us to call her whenever we wanted.

Then one day Kyeong Sook invited us to come visit her. We had not seen her since Jay's funeral. She was no longer living in California. When Gary and I arrived Kyeong Sook met us at the hotel where we were staying, with a big grin on her face.

"Where do you want to go for lunch?" she asked. "How about Korean food?" We climbed into her car, she cranked up the radio, and we got on the freeway and drove east. There was a quiet certainty about her that struck me immediately. She not only looked like a person who was used to being in charge, she looked like it would take a great deal to derail her.

"At first I didn't even realize we had a Koreatown here," Kyeong Sook said. "But I found Chinatown one day, so I knew there had to be a Koreatown too."

We turned onto a side street, parked the car and walked past a truck unloading a crate of green vegetables and plastic bags full of bean sprouts. At the restaurant a middle-aged woman greeted us.

"Long time no see," she said, "Where you been many days?"

Kyeong Sook looked embarrassed. "Working. My Mom and Dad are here visiting me." The women smiled. She eyed me curiously searching my face, looking me over. Leaning close to me she said, "Very good Korean daughter. Always she brings her American boyfriend to my restaurant."

"How is the fish today?" Kyeong Sook said, pointing to something on the menu.

The owner nodded and said, "The Sculpin is very fresh." She left and busied herself at the counter and returned to our table bearing a tray full of food.

"Something special," she said, setting down many small bowls filled with cucumber *kimchi*, radish *kimchi*, wrapped *kimchi*, and water *kimchi*.

"Eat," she said patting my arm, and pouring me more tea. We dipped tubu (it's called tofu in Japanese; and tubu in Korean) in a spicy red bean sauce, and as we ate steaming bowls of seaweed soup, Kyeong Sook smiled at me, and I smiled back. We finished our meal, ate our candied plums, and I thanked the restaurant proprietor in Korean, offering a slight bow with my head.

Kyeong Sook had reached adulthood taking pride in her Korean ancestry. She was wholly Americanized, fully assimilated into America with white friends and she had Asian friends. She was bicultural and able to shift from Korean to American with ease. But deep down she was Korean. Belonging to a Korean community was an ongoing aspect in her life, and wherever she chose to go from here, I knew that a part of her would always stay connected.

"C'mon." Kyeong Sook pulled me towards the door. "I want to take you somewhere else too." We cruised the shops and found isles of lacqueware inlaid with mother-of-pearl, rows of gleaming grayish green Celadon, and bargain bins of rhinestone barrettes. Some of the Asian women who worked in the shops came up to Kyeong Sook, saying, "Hi, long time no see." They exchanged smiles and chatted for a few minutes. Then we moved off through the crowd, following Kyeong Sook into the sunlight.

At the end of that day I kissed Kyeong Sook on the cheek, something I hadn't done since she was a child.

THE LAST DAY OF OUR VISIT, while I was at Kyeong Sook's apartment, she said, "Mom, I've got a big favor to ask, can you take my clothes out of the washing machine, and put them in the dryer? I'm late for work and I don't want everything to get wrinkled. Do you mind?"

Sorting through the tangle of jeans and underwear reminded me of the day I met my daughter for the first time in 1987, when she was ten-years-old; a live-wire pixie with flashing almond eyes and a deep belly laugh. And that flash-fire sense of mistrust that kept her heart sealed in plastic, and didn't allow her to get close to anyone.

The only clothes she had were the ones she'd come wearing. The first night home she pulled off her jeans and threw them into the dirty clothes hamper. I'd planned to take her shopping the next day to begin to assemble a wardrobe. Yet because she would need something clean to wear in the morning I decided to wash her clothes. Before I put her jeans and T-shirt into the washing machine, I held the little knit shirt she had said goodbye to Korea in, had traveled across the world wearing. It was steamy and smelled sweetly of sesame, ginger and garlic. The fragrance of the country and the people she left behind were melded into the fabric.

Folding Kyeong Sook's laundry reminded me that she was still out of reach to me, like the brass ring on the merry-go-round that I was always trying to catch. By the time she was twelve, she began doing all of her own laundry.

While Vanessa and Jay complained about having to wash their own clothes and mopped the floor with paper towels after over-filling the machine, Kyeong Sook welcomed laundry. She sailed through washing, drying, and folding without my assistance.

There were drawbacks to adopting a half-grown, independent, competent child; it meant she allowed me few opportunities to mother her. Then barely out of high school, and after only eight years together, Kyeong Sook moved out on her own and I never lived with her again.

I sat cross-legged on the floor with the pile of her clean clothes in my lap, sorting through its treasures as if stories could be released. Her knit skirts and pants were a size too large, so that no matter how many times they circled the dryer, everything fit loose on her rounded hips. I stroked her sweater, the same pale green as good jade. I brushed its silky knit with my fingertips and breathed in the textures and colors of her clothes, as if I were reading the words in a diary, trying to get to know my daughter who was filled with secrets and privacy.

Jay had always spilled the contents of his pockets onto the coffee table. Vanessa left a trail of gas receipts and sales slips on the table, and everything was always spread out across the bedroom floor, a residue, an update, journalizing her life. But Kyeong Sook kept everything put away, out of sight, locked tight beside her vulnerability. I didn't know anything about her except the things she chose to tell me.

All of a sudden I wished that something of hers remained unwashed. And then I saw the pillow and rumpled blankets on her bed. I buried my face in the sheets; inhaled the scent of her perfume, deodorant and perspiration. She is my daughter, and I am her mother, yet in some ways we are still just starting out.

# EPILOGUE

"But I've walked so many places in those shoes," five-year-old Jay said. "Do I have to get rid of them?"

"Aren't they too small for you?" I asked.

He shrugged, and then he hobbled towards me. "I can still fit into them, only I can't stretch out my toes."

Jay was a little boy who never wanted to part with his outgrown shoes.

"What about the pair you outgrew last summer, can we toss those out?"

"Mom!" Jay blinked up; his eyes were watery pools. He sat motionless for several moments, staring into his lap. I lifted him onto my knee, studied the gold flecks glittering in his tense dark eyes.

"OK, you can keep them." I agreed, and I scraped off some strawberry jam that had dried like a brilliant cut ruby on the toe of his shoe.

In time, Jay began collecting rare coins, and stamps. His hobby interest in old vintage cars developed, and he stopped saving his outgrown shoes. Yet the shoes of my son's life are a scrapbook in my mind: the light blue rubber baby shoes he arrived from Korea wearing, a first-grader with brand new school shoes, kicking them off to cuddle with me as I read to him. The boy with suntanned legs who fished mountain streams wearing knee-high rubber boots, the sleepy child who wrapped his arms around my neck, feet dangling.

And the new pair of tennis shoes Jay wore to Korea and then six months later walked out of the hospital wearing, to face a Hospice death at home, at age fifteen, days before his body finally wore out from cancer.

The night before he died, Jay loosened the laces and kicked his shoes off at the foot of his bed for the last time. Now those shoes stay in the closet and comfort me in long nights of remembering. I pick them up and press my hand into the place where my son's feet once stood. I stand quietly and remember waking him up in the morning and starting the day, sitting at the kitchen table together, cups of cocoa in hand, Jay's foot kicking the table leg while he told me about his latest favorite book. There were difficult moments too. Those shoes witnessed arguments and angry outbursts, but mostly they were surrounded by love and caring.

Years pass and still I keep Jay's shoes. Older grief is softer. It's about piercing pain channeled, reshaped and rounded into tender grace. I hold Jay's shoe and feel him smiling at me, running barefoot in my heart.

# ACKNOWLEDGMENTS

I owe thanks first to the folks at KAAN for their support of this memoir, and to Marcia Adams Ho, who did the cover art and understood the vision even before I did. Chris Winston not only represented me, she believed in me and had the foresight to place me with precisely the right editor, Grace Rachow. I'm grateful to Terri Sheridan, Brian Boyd, Bob Bensen, Dawn Downey, Kathy Beck, Maggie Dunham, Dawn Moore, Leslie Koda, and Larry Ho whose interest, advice, and inspiration were invaluable.

Most of all, I thank the members of my family who share this story. Vanessa, you are insightful and challenge me to think in new ways that constantly surprise me. Jay, I thank my lucky stars for the days I walked this earth with you. You are a fine teacher. Kyeong Sook, thank you for understanding the need to retell hard memories, and for giving me the encouragement I needed. Gary, you kept me afloat through every storm, often with humor too, and fed me wonderfully from the garden and the sea. My grandfather, Sharold Axton, gave me a lifetime of storytelling, and Bill Downey taught me how to get my stories on the page. Words cannot express my gratefulness to Bill for teaching me to trust my memories.

Help came in many forms. I would like to acknowledge my gratitude to the countless others who helped with this book. While your name is not listed you know who you are, and of the role you played, and I tenderly thank you.